TOOLS, TREASURES, & MEASURES

For Middle Grade Success

by Imogene Forte and Sandra Schurr

Incentive Publications, Inc.
Nashville, Tennessee

Edited by Jan Keeling and Leslie Britt
Cover by Marta Drayton
Illustrated by Marta Drayton

ISBN 0-86530-274-X

Overview

Table of Contents

USING A VARIETY OF STRATEGIES TO DIFFERENTIATE INSTRUCTION

ENCOURAGING THE DEVELOPMENT OF THINKING SKILLS ACROSS THE CURRICULUM

ASSESSING STUDENT INTERESTS, ABILITIES, AND GROWTH

PREFACE

Life in the middle level classroom is becoming more complicated each day. The growing emphasis on student-centered education has been embraced by dedicated middle grades educators who are working hard to implement new instructional strategies and organizational procedures to build a positive community for learning. Adding to the complexity are changing curricular and evaluation requirements of state and national legislation, which require a focus on a common set of student performance and assessment outcomes. To meet this challenge, educators are seeking not only a greater understanding of middle grades philosophy and research, but actual, usable, hands-on materials and methods that can help them to be effective in the middle grades classroom.

Tools, Treasures, & Measures, created as a practical companion to the comprehensive handbook *The Definitive Middle School Guide,* is a hands-on resource for busy teachers who want easy access to high-quality materials to help them improve classroom delivery systems. Containing effective teaching strategies and organizational techniques, dynamic activities and assignments, valuable assessment instruments and reporting systems, and lists, lesson plans, and inventories (plus an answer key and all-inclusive index), this book is a *living* source book, offering the teacher everything needed to capitalize on the middle school organizational pattern. Its five modules are related in content, but are organized so that each may be used independently for training purposes.

Module I, **Structuring the School Community To Accommodate Diversity and Commonalities,** offers materials to help with the exploration of issues such as cultural diversity, individual learning styles, student empowerment, parent involvement, and varied ability levels. Module II, **Encouraging the Development of Thinking Skills Across the Curriculum,** focuses on creative and critical thinking skills and presents models for "stretching the minds and teasing the imaginations" of students *and* teachers. Module III, **Using a Variety of Strategies To Differentiate Instruction,** introduces prototypes of a variety of ways to individualize classroom instruction—so that all students can learn. Module IV, **Making Sure They Are Taught—Not Caught— In the Middle,** provides teachers with multiple ways to modify and enrich the curriculum so that desired student outcomes can be achieved in all subject areas. Module V, **Assessing Student Interests, Abilities, and Growth,** outlines alternative ways for schools to measure student achievement, including product, performance, and portfolio assessment.

Each page is designated as a tool, a treasure, or a measure:

Tools
- Student activities
- Student assignments

Treasures
- Teacher information sheets
- Lesson plans

Measures
- Assessment instruments
- Assessment techniques

All are gathered into a dynamic presentation of topics and highly practical pages that teachers will use and cherish for years to come. Because of the increasing complexity of life in the middle level classroom; because of the changing demands of state and national legislation; because of the challenges of new evaluation methods; because of your desire for the most effective classroom delivery system; and, most of all, because of the diverse and changing needs of today's middle grades students: this book is your lifesaver!

STRUCTURING THE THE SCHOOL COMMUNITY TO ACCOMMODATE DIVERSITY AND COMMONALITIES

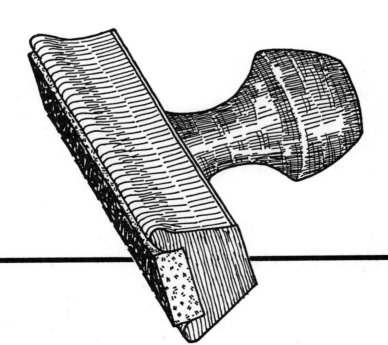

A "Quick Thinking" Self-Inventory

Without thinking for very long about the open-ended statements below, complete each one with the first thought that comes into your head:

1. **Adults are usually** _____

_____

2. **Most of the time I think teachers are** _____

_____

3. **The biggest problem I have with people of my own age is** _____

_____

4. **My classmates are more impressed by** _____

_____

5. **I think my classmates see me as** _____

_____

6. **The thing I like most about school is** _____

_____

7. **One thing I would like to change about the world today is** _____

_____

8. **Things that cause prejudice and misunderstandings are** _____

_____

9. **One thing I really like about my community is** _____

_____

10. **One thing I would like to change is** _____

_____

11. **I would like to be more** _____

_____

12. **Someone I really admire is** _____
    because _____
13. **I think writing answers to questions like this is** _____

_____

After you have finished writing answers to all the questions, go back to question number one and read all your answers. Is there something you could learn about yourself by pondering your answers? If you like, add the completed work to your journal or portfolio for later reflection and discuss your feelings about the activity with the teacher.

Observation Orientation

People-watching is a fascinating hobby! It can help us develop a keener awareness of the marvelous sense of diversity within the human race and at the same time deepen our appreciation of the commonalities shared by all.

To help you develop your observation skills and to become better acquainted with your classmates, complete each of the sentences below. Try not to use any person's name more than once.

1. The name of the person who appears to be the tallest boy in our class is _____.
   The name of the boy who appears to be the next tallest is _____.

2. The girl who is sitting nearest to the classroom door is _____.

3. The name of a girl who has blue eyes is _____.
   Speaking of eyes, the name of a boy with brown eyes is _____.

4. The full name of one person who wears glasses is _____.

5. The names of two people who are wearing shoes of the same color are _____
   and _____. ____ other people in the room are wearing shoes of this color.

6. _____ is wearing a shirt with buttons.

7. A person I admire a lot is wearing _____.

8. _____ impresses me as being a very hard worker.

9. The person wearing an article of clothing I would like to own is _____.
   The article of clothing is _____.

10. The name of the person who appears to have the longest hair is _____.

11. _____ is a person who impresses me as being very cheerful and outgoing and very well adjusted to school.

12. Since I have been observing my classmates in order to complete this activity, the name of the person I have seen smile the most is _____.

Name _____

Consensual Conclusions:

Using Cooperative Learning Groups To Aid in Reaching Consensual Conclusions

The Jury Is Out!

Ask students to work in cooperative learning groups to find consensual conclusions for the following situations. Each group will need to consider the situations and determine its own approach to reaching a consensual conclusion. Strategies to consider might include:

- **discussion**
- **questioning**
- **debate**
- **deliberation**
- **surveying**
- **polling**
- **petitioning**
- **argument**
  and
- **persuasion.**

The object of the activity is to reach some conclusion upon which each group member can agree. In the event that this objective becomes impossible to achieve, the group should compromise by cooperating to write a brief summary of the group's efforts, including an analysis of the points of disagreement and suggestions for new approaches to reaching consensus, even if it involves some degree of compromise.

Consensual Conclusions:

Situation 1

A school sports team is found guilty of breaking game rules and cheating during an intramural tournament. After careful investigation, it is determined that the captain and several other team members were opposed to the decision to cheat and tried to convince the team to observe the rules of the game. When outvoted by a majority of the team members, they elected to allow the "majority to rule" and support the cheating. A proposal to disqualify team members from participation in school intramurals for the remainder of the school year has been placed before the school administrators. The intramural committee has proposed three alternative plans for consideration.

Determine the fairest and most fitting conclusion (reach group consensus on one of the following conclusions).

CONCLUSIONS

_____ **1.** Disqualify all members of the team from participation in intramural activities for the remainder of the school year.

_____ **2.** Disqualify only the members of the team who supported the cheating. Allow the members who voted against cheating to join other teams and resume playing.

_____ **3.** Ask each member of the team to do three hours of school community service, to write an essay on the value of honesty and fair play, and to meet with a teacher, coach, or school counselor to discuss team responsibility. Then allow all to participate fully in all intramural activities.

Group _____

Consensual Conclusions:

Situation 2

A social studies teacher in your school has a gender bias that is reflected in class discussions, in assigning group responsibilities, and even in grading. This particular teacher is actually insulting and unfair to one particular group of students. Everyone hates to admit that this is true, but it has become very difficult to ignore.

Determine the fairest and most fitting conclusion.

CONCLUSIONS

_____ **1.** Draft a student petition calling the teacher's attention to the situation and asking for a change in attitude and behavior. Get signatures from all members of the class if possible.

_____ **2.** Report the situation to the principal and ask to have someone from the administration talk with the teacher.

_____ **3.** Ignore the situation and hope that the teacher will change, or realize that the school year won't last forever and conclude that it's really not the students' problem.

Group _____

21

Situation 3

One student in your class picks on and makes fun of any class members he considers "different." He makes up derogatory names for them, laughs at their mistakes, and publicly makes fun of the way they dress and/or speak. This kid can be really cruel. The whole class is irritated with his behavior and wants to put an end to it.

Determine the fairest and most fitting conclusion.

CONCLUSIONS

_____ **1.** The student should be confronted by several members of the class and asked to consider the effects of his negative behavior.

_____ **2.** Class members singled out by this student should report the behavior to the teacher and ask for intervention.

_____ **3.** A letter should be written to the belittling student detailing the class members' distaste for his insensitive behavior, and requesting that it cease immediately.

Group _____

Personally Speaking

Complete the following sentences about reading to help your teacher do a better job of planning reading-related activities for you.

1. I think books are _____.

2. I like to read about _____.

3. The last book I read was _____.

4. My favorite author is _____.

5. I think teachers should ___ or should not ___ assign specific books for students to read.

6. I think our school library is _____.

7. I think my reading skills are excellent ___ average ___ or poor___.

8. Long books are _____.

9. Newspapers and magazines _____.

10. My favorite place to read is _____.

11. On a scale of 1 to 4 (1 being the best):
I like to read fiction ___ biography ___ how-to books ___ factual books ___.

12. If I could change anything I wanted to about our school reading program, I would
_____.

13. Most books written for students my age _____.

14. I think book reports are _____.

15. My favorite book in the whole world is _____.

Name _____

Multicultural Booklist To Promote Understanding and Appreciation of Diversity and Commonalities

The following bibliography of multicultural works of fiction was compiled and distributed by Judy Bulow and others in the children's department of The Tattered Cover bookstore in Denver, Colorado. All of the books on this list were included as appropriate for ages 12 and up and are grouped by area of the world. Many of the titles are new; some are not. They were selected to present books that best represent a multicultural society and to help youngsters gain an understanding of cultural and ethnic differences. All of these titles should be readily available in libraries and/or on the shelves of local bookstores.

• • •

Cross Cultural

The Brave by Robert Lipsyte
A Gathering of Flowers by Joyce Carol Thomas
The Return by Sonia Levitin

• • •

African-American

The Contender by Robert Lipsyte
Just Like Martin by Ossie Davis
Letters from a Slave Girl: The Story of Harriet Jacobs by Mary E. Lyons
Long Journey Home by Julius Lester
Maniac Magee by Jerry Spinelli
Nightjohn by Gary Paulsen
Road to Memphis by Mildred Taylor
Roll of Thunder, Hear My Cry by Mildred Taylor
Scorpions by Walter Dean Myers
Trouble's Child by Mildred Pitts Walter
Two Tickets to Freedom by Florence Freedman

• • •

West Indian and Caribbean

Ajeemah and His Son by James Berry
Annie John by Jamaica Kincaid
A Taste of Salt: A Story of Modern Haiti by Frances Temple

• • •

South Africa

Chain of Fire by Beverley Naidoo
Paper Bird by Maretha Maartens
Somehow Tenderness Survives by Hazel Rochman
Waiting for the Rain by Sheila Gordon

Mexico, Central And South America

The Crossing by Gary Paulsen
Journey of the Sparrows by Fran L. Buss
Lupita Mañana by Patricia Beatty
Taking Sides by Gary Soto

• • •

Native American

Calico Captive by Elizabeth Speare
Circle Unbroken by Sollace Hotze

• • •

Asian

Children of the River by Linda Crew
Homesick: My Own Story by Jean Fritz
Song of the Buffalo Boy by Sherry Garland
Year of Impossible Goodbyes by Sook Nyul Choi

• • •

Middle East

Kiss the Dust by Elizabeth Laird
One More River by Lynn Reid Banks
Shabanu, Daughter of the Wind by Suzanne Fisher Staples

• • •

Additional Titles Of Special Merit Related To The Holocaust

Devil's Arithmetic by Jane Yolen
The Journey Back by Johanna Reiss

Organize a "Meet and Greet" Program for Your School

Consider adapting the community Welcome Wagon concept to the school setting as a way to involve parents and students new to the school.

Each new family should be given a "Meet and Greet" Bag containing coupons that are "cashed in" for freebies or goodies which provide them with opportunities to meet a number of key people and programs in the school.

The "Meet and Greet" Bag should be personalized with the school's name printed on it and should contain a wide range of coupons, informational flyers, directories of community resources, and special forms/announcements to acquaint family members with the school and the community it represents.

Students are encouraged to cash in all coupons, examine all flyers, meet all school personnel, and complete all activities as soon as possible. This helps the boys and girls get involved early in their adjustment period.

New students can be asked to stand up in front of their homeroom classes and announce their names and the places from which they moved.

If your school is fortunate enough to receive the support of a strong parent organization, each new household can be assigned a "buddy family" and personal contact should be made. Recruiting of volunteers and encouraging family involvement in school projects are the goals of this initial contact.

A personal contact should also be made by the school's administration, either by mail or by telephone. An invitation to visit the school can be offered at this time.

The monthly school newsletter to parents might offer a regular column called "WHO'S NEW" that identifies all incoming families to the school population and perhaps highlights regional areas from which these families have moved.

On the whole, the "Meet and Greet" project is a joint effort by all representative populations at your school—parents, students, teachers, and administrators. New kids and parents should indeed find out what makes your school special and the "Meet and Greet" vehicle is one way to do it!

P.S. Patterns for selected coupons for you to enlarge and reproduce are included on the following "MEET AND GREET STARTER KIT" pages.

How To Implement a "Meet and Greet" Program in Your School

The following outline provides you with a detailed plan for implementing a "Meet and Greet" Program in your school. Follow these steps and procedures for a successful program to help your new students feel at home from the first day on.

1. Organize a local "Meet and Greet" Advisory Board for your school. The purpose of this group is to:
    a. select coupon items for the "Meet and Greet" Bag.
    b. select and collect additional community resource information for the "Meet and Greet" Bag.
    c. organize a pool of people to assemble "Meet and Greet" Bags, distribute "Meet and Greet" Bags, and to contact parents of students receiving "Meet and Greet" Bags.

2. Establish overall budget (and raise funding if necessary) for "Meet and Greet" Bags. Do you want a $2.00 bag, a $3.00 bag, or a $10.00 bag?

3. Determine who will receive "Meet and Greet" Bags. Options include:
    a. all students new to school.
    b. only students new to community, county, or state.
    c. all first-year or incoming students.

4. Survey the community to obtain quantities of other free items and information bulletins that would be of help to families moving into the school district.

5. Assemble "Meet and Greet" Bags, including coupons and items collected from the school and/or community.

6. Promote your program through press releases to local media—radio, television, and news media.

7. Set up a distribution plan for "Meet and Greet" Bags. Consider giving out new student registers at the same time.

8. Compile a weekly (or monthly if preferred) list of all new students and make it available to the Parent-Teacher Organization for follow-up telephone calls to the home.

9. Have fun and enjoy your exciting "Meet and Greet" Program!

Suggested Contents of "Meet and Greet" Bag

I. COUPONS

The following coupons with their corresponding items make up the major contents of the "Meet and Greet" Bag. Each school should select those coupon items best suited for the geographic location, student population, special interests, and allocated budget of its school community.

Most commercial coupon-related items can be ordered directly from a local vendor dealing in sales/promotional items. The Yellow Pages will provide you with the names and addresses of several options listed under either Advertising Specialties or Promotional Advertising. It is suggested that appropriate items (such as pencils, rulers, bookmarks, key chains, magnets, etc.) be personalized with the name of the elementary, middle, or junior high school.

	COUPONS	SUGGESTED COPY	PROMOTIONAL ITEM
1.	Cookie	Meet the Cafeteria Gang. Cash in for FREE Cookie!	Cookie
2.	Pencil	Meet the School Secretary. Cash in for FREE Pencil!	Pencil
3.	Bookmark	Meet the Media Specialist. Cash in for FREE Bookmark!	Bookmark
4.	Ruler	Meet the Art Teacher. Cash in for FREE Ruler!	Ruler
5.	Frisbee/Spinning Top	Meet the P.E. Teacher. Cash in for FREE Frisbee!	Frisbee/Spinning Top
6.	Whistle	Meet the Music Teacher. Cash in for FREE Whistle!	Whistle
7.	Key Chain	Meet the Principal. Cash in for FREE Key Chain!	Key Chain
8.	Litter Bag	Meet the Custodian. Cash in for FREE Litter Bag!	Litter Bag
9.	Adhesive Strip	Meet the School Nurse. Cash in for FREE Adhesive Strip!	Adhesive Strip
10.	Bumper Sticker	Meet the Bus Driver. Cash in for FREE Bumper Sticker!	Bumper Sticker

It should also be noted that coupons can be cashed in for school-related services or activities rather than specific products. Some examples include:

	SHAPE OF COUPON	COPY	SERVICE ACTIVITIES
1.	Apple	Meet the Principal. Cash in for Special Lunch!	Lunch with the principal
2.	Telephone	Meet the Teacher. Cash in for FREE Phone Call to your home!	Warm fuzzy telephone call to the home during the first week of school
3.	Newspaper	Meet the School Newspaper sponsor. Cash in for FREE copy of Next Issue!	Issue of School Newspaper
4.	Tee Shirt	Meet the Parent-Teacher Organization. Cash in for $1.00 off School Tee Shirt!	$1.00 Off School Tee Shirt
5.	Bus	Meet the Bus Driver. Cash in for seat of your choice!	Sit in seat of choice for one week

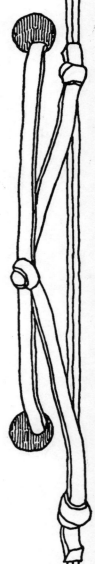

II. COMMUNITY REFERENCE/RESOURCE ITEMS

It is also important to include a variety of reference materials or resources that are both school- and community-related. Introducing newcomers to the school community is very important to any new family's orientation. Some free and available items to collect and include for this purpose might be:

A. School-related Materials
1. School Map
2. School Newsletter
3. School Calendar
4. Name/Address of Brownie/Scout Leaders
5. School Annual Report
6. School Handbook of Student Conduct

B. Community-related Materials
1. City Map
2. Library Card Application for Public Library
3. Names/Addresses of Local Physicians/Dentists
4. Names/Addresses of Local Day Care Centers
5. Names/Addresses of Local Adult Education Programs
6. Names/Addresses of Local Recreation Department Programs
7. Bike Reflectors from AAA
8. Information on Local Substance Abuse Program

SUGGESTED PATTERNS FOR "MEET AND GREET" COUPONS

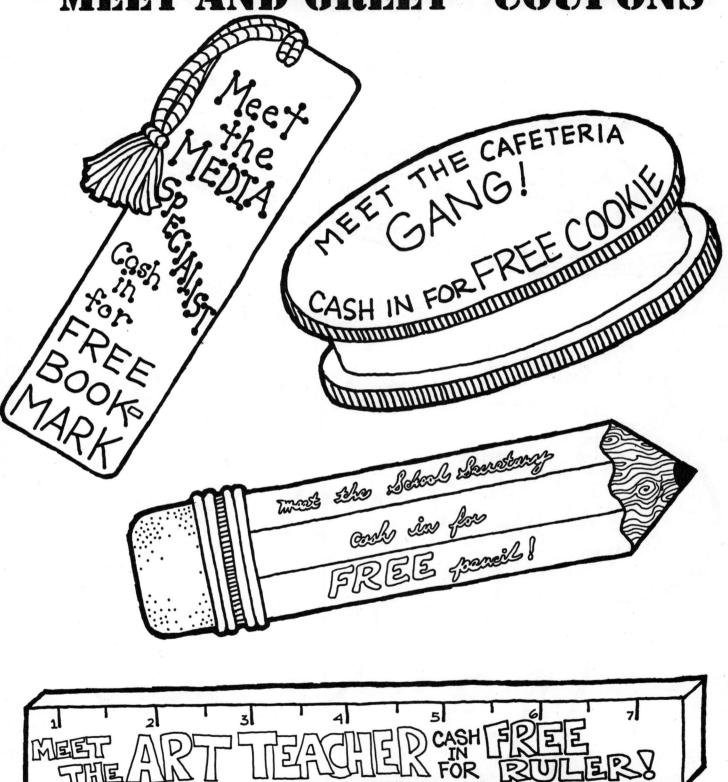

Meet the MEDIA SPECIALIST

Cash in for FREE BOOK MARK

MEET THE CAFETERIA GANG! CASH IN FOR FREE COOKIE

meet the School Secretary cash in for FREE pencil!

MEET THE ART TEACHER CASH IN FOR FREE RULER!

SUGGESTED PATTERNS FOR "MEET AND GREET" COUPONS

SUGGESTED PATTERNS FOR "MEET AND GREET" COUPONS

meet the Principal

Cash in for a Special Lunch

MEET THE bus driver CASH IN FOR free Bumper Sticker

MEET THE CUSTODIAN CASH IN FOR FREE LITTER BAG

Keep America Clean

Meet the School Nurse cash in for FREE Adhesive Strip

SUGGESTED PATTERNS FOR "MEET AND GREET" COUPONS

SCHOOL BUS

MEET THE BUS DRIVER
Cash in for the
seat of your choice!

#31

NEWS

Meet the School
NEWSPAPER SPONSOR
cash in for
FREE copy of NEXT ISSUE

Meet the
PTA
cash in for
$1.00 off
School tee-shirt

Meet the TEACHER!
cash in for
FREE phone call home

Parents Are People, Too

Tips for Understanding Parents

It is important to remember "where parents are coming from" when they visit the classroom or call the school to express a concern, a complaint, or a criticism. Sometimes, just pausing to reflect on the factors that influence their behavior and attitudes towards you can help to defuse a situation with an angry, tired, or frustrated parent/guardian.

1. **Parents have their own perceptions and misperceptions of what schools should be like based on a variety of personal events, including:**
   a. Their own adolescent experiences
   b. Their own family relationships
   c. Their own fears and frustrations
   d. Their own hopes and expectations
   e. Their own personalities and learning styles
   f. Their own interactions with teachers and schooling

2. **Parents also have several personal needs which are likely to carry over from the home or workplace to the school, including:**
   a. A need to assert power and control over their children
   b. A need to feel needed
   c. A need to impress friends, relatives, or neighbors
   d. A need to appease the other parent
   e. A need to assert independence over authority in school

3. **Parents often face several stressful life events which can affect their ability to deal rationally with problems in school according to "The Life Event Scale," a measure developed by Dr. Thomas Holmes and Dr. Richard Raahe. These stressful life events are:**
    a. Death of spouse or loved one in immediate family
    b. Divorce
    c. Marital separation
    c. Death of a close family member
    d. Major personal injury or illness
    e. Marriage
    e. Being fired or laid off of work
    f. Major change in health or behavior of family member
    g. Sexual difficulties
    h. Gaining a new family member

4. **Finally, parents must continually overcome these three emotional barriers which tend to interfere with their support roles of school age children when faced with conflict or change:**
    a. Parental frustration with the child's changing developmental stages and conflicting behavior phases
    b. Parental fears about the child's ability to "make it" in today's culturally diverse society and world of technology
    c. Parental ambitions for what a child should accomplish as a student and ultimately become as an adult

Tips for Helping Parents and Students Work Together for Learning Success

FOR STUDENTS TO CONSIDER:

1. Try sitting in the front row or near the front row in each of your classes because:
   a. You can hear and see the teacher better.
   b. You will more likely be surrounded by ambitious students.
   c. You are less likely to get bored.
   d. You are more likely to pay attention and get involved in the class activity.
   e. You are more likely to give the teacher a better chance to know you in a positive light.
2. Dress appropriately and use "good taste" in your grooming because one tends to act and behave the way one looks and talks.
3. Sit up and pay attention to what the teacher is saying because teachers appreciate positive feedback and are more likely to improve their delivery of information.
4. Always have something to "read or write" in class for the times when there is nothing else to do. This will make it less easy for you to get into trouble or bother others who are still working.
5. Volunteer to answer a question or help out the teacher when asked to do so since teachers appreciate a considerate offer especially when it is unexpected.
6. Be sure to thank your teacher for helping you because good deeds often come around again.

FOR PARENTS TO CONSIDER:

1. Try to avoid unnecessary and unexpected absences and lateness which complicate the busy teacher's schedule.
2. Be sure to complete and return all classroom/school forms and signed notices promptly.
3. Help establish a study time, routine, and location at home for your child so that school becomes a priority from the very beginning.
4. Get in the habit of sending "thank you notes and warm fuzzies" to the teacher when appropriate to do so.
5. Support the teacher in all problem situations with your child by responding immediately to requests for conferences, help, or shared solutions.
6. Establish a means for getting your child organized in the morning before school so that he or she leaves the house "ready for work" and with everything that is needed "to get the job done."

Getting To Know You

A Collaborative Inventory for Students and Their Parents To Complete

DIRECTIONS: Please take a few minutes to complete this "Getting To Know You" conference form. I will be scheduling a visit with you soon to discuss the information so that we can cooperatively plan for a productive school year.

Student's Name _____ Date _____

Parent/Guardian's Name(s): _____

1. My child has the following interests, hobbies, and extracurricular activities outside of school: _____
_____

2. My child's biggest strengths and successes in school seem to be:_____
_____
_____

3. One thing my child worries most about in school is: _____
_____
_____

4. My child works well with teachers who:_____
_____
_____

5. If you have to discipline my child in school, my child and I prefer that you (check all that apply):
   _____ Use a time-out chair/room   _____ Scold (not in so nice a way)
   _____ Lecture (in a nice way)   _____ Administer grounding at home or school
   _____ Take away school/home privileges   _____ Contact the home immediately and leave discipline to us
   _____ Other (please specify) _____
   _____

6. The most important thing we all want from this year's schooling experience is: _____
_____

7. The best times/days for a parent/student/teacher conference is: _____
_____

Signed: _____ Signed: _____
    Parent/Guardian   Student

Measures for Dealing with Parent Problems

DIRECTIONS: Consider your situation. Decide how each of the following seven parent-related frustrations relates to your present job. Put an "x" on the line to show the level of frequency of the problem in your normal job responsibilities.

1. Others blame you for your parent problems over which you have no control.

|--|

Does not happen frequently   Happens frequently

2. Parents pressure you with last-minute requests.

|--|

Does not happen frequently   Happens frequently

3. People who do not understand your job make parent-related decisions that strongly affect your work.

|--|

Does not happen frequently   Happens frequently

4. People don't give you the right parent-related information or materials you need to do your job.

|--|

Does not happen frequently   Happens frequently

5. People inside the organization do not cooperate with you when you want to serve parents.

|--|

Does not happen frequently   Happens frequently

6. Parents change their expectations once a job is underway.

|--|

Does not happen frequently   Happens frequently

7. People you depend on do not do their parent-related jobs correctly.

|--|

Does not happen frequently   Happens frequently

NOW . . . discuss these frustrations with your colleagues and brainstorm a list of positive actions that can be taken to minimize their impact in your classroom.

Personal Review of a Parent Challenge To Use as a Tool for Growth

Think about a situation when you were dealing with an upset parent or guardian during which you took things personally. Describe it in the spaces provided below.

1. What were the specifics?

THE PEOPLE _____
_____
_____

WHAT WAS SAID _____
_____
_____

THE SETTING _____
_____
_____

THE TIMING _____
_____
_____

OTHER FACTORS _____
_____
_____

HOW IT TURNED OUT _____
_____
_____

2. List things you said or did—after you lost your patience with the parent—that you would do differently next time. _____
_____
_____
_____

3. Make a list of three things you can start doing right now to become a more positive person in dealing with parents and guardians. _____
_____
_____
_____

Team/Student/Parent Conference Form

Student's Name: _____ Date: _____

Reason for Conference: _____

_____

_____

_____

Parent Concerns: _____

_____

_____

_____

Teacher Concerns: _____

_____

_____

_____

Student Concerns: _____

_____

_____

_____

Plan: 1) _____

_____

    2) _____

_____

    3) _____

_____

Signatures: _____
             Team Representative or Advisor

         _____
             Parent

         _____
             Student

Next Conference or Follow-up: _____

Ten Parent Involvement Strategies That Work

1. **Mutual Goal Setting, Contracting, and Evaluating**

   In September, send a letter home that clearly states your parent involvement goals for the coming months. Include confirmation of these goals through support statements from teachers.

   Ask each student to write a personal hand-written comment at the bottom of the letter before it goes home, encouraging the family to take advantage of this opportunity to help build the bridge between home and school.

   Throughout the year, follow up this initial letter with a self-evaluation progress report to parents summarizing the events or activities that have supported these mutual goals.

2. **Assessment of School Policies, Practices, and Rituals**

   Analyze whether and how the school does or does not welcome parents into its schooling process.

   Often principals are not aware of the many standard routines, policies, and procedures within any school that might intimidate or "turn off" parents. These factors range from informal messages such as "Visitors Must Report to the Office" to more formal actions such as assigning out-of-school suspension for students who need in-school attention.

   As Johnston (1990) suggests, educators might conduct a "family impact assessment" of their schools to determine which things are being done consciously or unconsciously to limit parental or student access to the "eyes and ears" of the faculty.

3. **Parent Lounge/Center/Resource Room**

   Set up a special parent lounge/center/resource room for use by the school community.

   Everybody likes to have a "gathering place" where they can relate to their peers, socialize with their compatriots, or learn from their counterparts. Parents are no exception.

Providing parents with a part of the school facility that they can call their own is very effective in drawing them into the building and involving them in the business of educating their offspring.

Such parent accommodations need not be elaborate but should feature such things as access to a pot of coffee, to a lending library of parenting aids, to a display of social service/agency information pamphlets, and to a cadre of parents who will share their wisdom and experiences. One creative organizer of a parent center included a portable school supply cart and an organized toy, sporting goods, and clothing exchange.

4. Public Information Display, Public Service Messages, and Work Site Seminars

Spend more time taking school programs and politics out into the community rather than expecting the parent community to meet only on school turf and time. These outreach efforts can result in increased parental support and input.

Administrators might try setting up a series of public parent program displays in the local supermarkets, shopping malls, medical centers, or community agency offices to promote the importance of parent partnerships in student achievement.

Regular public service messages over the local radio and television stations can reinforce the idea of building bridges to build better schools. Another idea is to conduct short but meaningful parent workshops or seminars at major parent job sites during the lunch periods or evening hours. This is cost effective and time effective for the parents in busy working families.

5. Weekend or Evening Public Information Fair

Stage a public fair during an evening or on a weekend to educate community members about all aspects of schooling and the potential influences community members can have on student achievement. The fair could resemble a carnival, with booths featuring informational displays by various community agencies or presentations by professional speakers who share their educational expertise in a roundtable discussion.

Individual school faculty members and program sponsors can set up booths to show off student work and projects or demonstrate application of self-help learning tips that can be used at home or in school.

Complimentary refreshments and free baby-sitting services should also be provided to make it both attractive and convenient.

6. Parent and Student Exchange Day

Initiate a Parent and Student Exchange Day. Sometimes parents have little appreciation for either the demands on the student in school or the demands on the teacher in the classroom. Allowing parents to come to school in place of their children for one day to experience firsthand the complexities of the educational process can be a real eye opener.

Encourage parents to ride the school bus, eat in the school cafeteria, attend classes, and complete the assigned homework for the day.

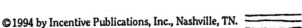

This activity can be based on an open invitation to parents to attend on a day of their choice, or it can be on a designated parent exchange day. The ultimate goal, of course, is to make parents aware of the important things that go on in school so they can support both the teacher and the student in a more meaningful and knowledgeable way.

7. Parent Involvement
Encourage parents to commit some time or energy to the school. For example, the school might generate a menu of desirable parent involvement activities such as:
• Take your child to the public library once a week this marking period.
• Attend at least one "How To Help My Child Learn" workshop during the semester.
• Keep a shared success journal with your child with at least five entries this month.
• Complete at least one family activity suggested on the School Calendar of Good Family Times this week.
• Attend one Parent-Teacher Organization meeting this semester.
• Limit television viewing for your child to no more than 10 hours this week and substitute something of your own choosing in its place.
• Visit the Parent Resource Center at the school and write the principal a personal note commenting on the experience.

8. An Old-Fashioned Family Night at School
Sponsor an old-fashioned family night as a way to bring parents to school (Torney, 1990). Torney stresses that most parents need a sense of community, need to know they are good parents, need to know who their kids' friends are, and want to support a program that helps them parent.

Her formula for "pulling off such an event" dictates that the participants have something to look at (student work), something to listen to (student entertainment), something to be recognized for (student awards), something to laugh about (student skits/demonstrations/role playing), and something to talk about (student/parent discussion groups).

9. Parent/Teacher Dialogue Journals for Communication
Encourage parents and teachers to maintain dialogue journals. This process need not be complicated or time-consuming if it is implemented correctly.

Teachers might initiate this activity by following the advice of Jane Baskwell (1987) who sends home a simple stapled booklet of empty pages at the beginning of the school year, along with a letter that suggests parents take a few minutes to jot down questions, anecdotes, or comments about anything related to their child.

When they have recorded something, parents send the booklet back to school with the child and the teacher responds accordingly. No pressure is placed on the parent to comply, although the teacher might initiate a dialogue with selected parents by sending the first entry.

Principals can facilitate this process by providing interested teachers with inexpensive journal booklets complete with school logo and colors. They might also try using dialogue journals with their own staff members as an in-house communication tool.

 ©1994 by Incentive Publications, Inc., Nashville, TN.

10. Monthly Home Achievement Packets

Organize a series of monthly parent Home Achievement Packets to be used to train parents in ways to help their children at home. Parents whose primary language is not English, or parents with a limited educational background, are often reluctant to participant in school-based learning workshops because they feel inadequate.

One way to address this problem is to structure a series of take-home learning centers that contain an audio- or videotape of simple information/instructions/problems, a script of the material presented on the tape, a list of related activities to do with the student, and even an article or two on the topic for parents to read or listen to (again in tape format).

Monthly topics for these Home Achievement Packets might include:

1. How To Set Up a Study Area
2. How To Organize Family Field Trips in the Community
3. How To Select a College or Trade School
4. How To Access Community Agencies
5. How To Reduce Test Anxiety
6. How To Improve Your Child's Study Skills
7. How To Make the Most of a Parent Conference
8. How To Discipline Your Adolescent
9. How To Say "No" to Your Children
10. How To Handle Conflict in the Home

References:

Baskwell, Jane. *Parents and Teachers: Partners in Learning*. New York: Scholastic Inc., 1989.

Berla, Nancy; Henderson, Ann T.; and Kerewsky, William. *The Middle School Years: A Parents' Handbook*. Columbia, Md.: National Committee for Citizens in Education, 1989.

Conners, Neila A. *Homework*. Columbus, Ohio: National Middle School Association, 1991.

Epstein, Joyce L. "Paths to Partnership: What We Can Learn from Federal, State, District, and School Initiatives." *Phi Delta Kappan*. January 1991.

Johnston, J. Howard. *The New American Family and the School*. Columbus, Ohio: National Middle School Association, 1990.

Schurr, Sandra L. "Don't Just Welcome New Students—Meet and Greet Them!" *Middle School Journal*. May 1987.

Torney, Pat. "Family Night Brings Parents to School." *Middle School Journal*. November 1990.

Williams, David L. and Chavkin, Nancy Feyl. "Essential Elements of Strong Parent Involvement Programs." *Educational Leadership*. October 1989.

Adapted from "Fine Tuning Your Parent Power Increases Student Achievement" by Sandra L. Schurr. *Schools in the Middle: Theory into Practice*. Reston, VA: NASSP. Vol. 2, no. 2. Winter 1992. Used by permission.

Creative Homework Assignments To Challenge Bored Minds and Compete with TV Sitcoms

Instead of assigning two pages of math problems straight from the textbook, the language workbook lesson for the day, or finding answers for the questions at the end of the social studies chapter, surprise your students with one of these unusual homework assignments:

1. Listen to the local news on TV or the radio. Select one event of interest to the community and write a brief summary of the information included in the newscast. Then write a paragraph telling how you think the event will affect the community, your family, and your school.

2. Ask students to write a simple play exploring some aspect of the current unit of study underway in the classroom. Share the plays and allow the group to vote to determine the best one. Produce the prize-winning play (if time permits) and allow the author to serve as director. (See Play Outline on page 48.)

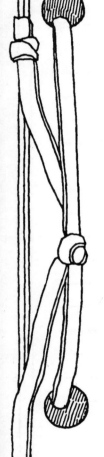

3. Read an extra chapter in your current library book and make a list of twenty interesting words from the chapter. Try to list some new words whose meanings you don't know and look them up in the dictionary.

4. Write a letter to the teacher outlining a unit of study that you think would be interesting for the class. Give good reasons to support your topic of choice and name some activities you would like to see incorporated into the unit.

5. Make a diorama or collage to illustrate a favorite book that you have just completed. Be creative and try to show as much of the book's flavor as possible.

6. Plan and set up a science experiment. Report your findings to the class at the end of a specified time. (See experiment form for use with any science topic on pages 49–50.)

7. Create a puzzle or game related to a topic being studied at the current time. (For examples of puzzle and game forms, see pages 92–102.)

8. Complete a mini-mini-unit on a topic being studied at the time. (For mini-mini-unit outline and samples, see pages 197–200.)

9. Take a whole week to complete the content-based mind-stretching unit on your own. Set a specific time for class culmination and discussion of the unit activities. (For mini-unit outline and sample, see pages 194–196.)

10. Design and create a poster to promote school spirit, class pride, or some school-wide campaign underway at the time. Bring the poster to class to be added to a classwide display.

Play
Outline
Ocean Adventures

Write a one-act play from a ship captain's point of view about an adventure taking place on a luxury cruise ship during a transatlantic voyage. Include information relating to parts of the ship, principles of ocean travel, roles of different workers, daily schedules, the influence of weather conditions and shipboard facilities, routines, and customs.

Create some captivating characters, develop an exciting plot, and make your play as interesting as possible.

Characters: _____

_____

_____

_____

Time and Place (Setting): _____

_____

_____

_____

Problem, Conflict, or Situation: _____

_____

_____

_____

Sequence of Events: _____

_____

_____

_____

Conflict Resolution/Climax: _____

_____

_____

_____

Special Words, Terms, and Information To Be Used: _____

_____

_____

_____

Name _____

Experiment Form
for Use with any Science Topic

KNOWLEDGE

List the materials used in this experiment.

Materials: _____

_____

_____

_____

_____

COMPREHENSION

Outline the procedure for conducting this experiment.
Procedure:

1. _____
2. _____
3. _____
4. _____
5. _____
6. _____

APPLICATION

Record data observed and collected during your experiment in chart or graph form.
Data:

What I Did	What I Observed

Name _____

From *Science Mind Stretchers* by Imogene Forte and
Sandra Schurr. Nashville, TN: Incentive Publications, 1987.

Experiment Form, Page 2

ANALYSIS

Examine your data and draw conclusions.

Conclusions:

1. _____
   _____

2. _____
   _____

3. _____
   _____

SYNTHESIS

Create a series of "what if" statements about your data to show things that might be different should variables be changed.

What if . . . _____
_____

What if . . . _____
_____

What if . . . _____
_____

EVALUATION

Describe how you would rate the success of your experiment. Establish a set of criteria for measuring the results.

Findings	Measure of Success

From *Science Mind Stretchers* by Imogene Forte and Sandra Schurr. Nashville, TN: Incentive Publications, 1987.

Ten Ways To Encourage a Learning Environment at Home

Use this simple checklist to determine whether you are doing everything you can to provide a learning environment for your child at home.

_____ **1.** Do all family members share in the household roles and responsibilities, helping one another out on a need basis?

_____ **2.** Does the family try to maintain some type of schedule for members of the family to eat, sleep, play, and work together as much as our busy lifestyle allows?

_____ **3.** Have we made it clear to all family members that school is an important priority for all of us?

_____ **4.** Do the family members share in one another's success stories as well as the burdens of one another's mistakes?

_____ **5.** Does every family member have his or her own place to work, study, read, or engage in learning activities?

_____ **6.** Does the family plan regular outings to community museums, libraries, historical sites, concerts, and other places of interest?

_____ **7.** Does the family limit television viewing and encourage reading among all members?

_____ **8.** Does the family find time to talk and debrief one another on what they are doing at school, work, and play on a daily or weekly basis?

_____ **9.** Do family members practice good speaking and listening habits using their best speech habits and learning new ones?

_____**10.** Does the family look forward to the future and find ways to plan for lifelong learning experiences?

Community Service Projects for Students

It is important that today's students be connected or re-connected with the institutions and individuals that make up their communities. In well-designed service learning programs, students do more than "visit nursing homes and clean up littered beaches." They apply what they've learned in the classroom, develop leadership and communication skills, become more caring and responsible citizens, and help meet community needs in the process.

Below is a list of service learning activities that are diverse and that can be effective with students at the middle level.

1. Organize a recycling program for your school.
2. Teach environmental awareness to younger students.
3. Look after "latchkey" children.
4. Plan a fun event for children at a hospital, foster home, or orphanage.
5. Start a community service club at school.
6. Begin a "book swap store" for your class.
7. Create art for a nursing home, hospital, or daycare center.
8. Start a cultural awareness club at school.
9. Have party guests bring supplies for the homeless or underprivileged rather than a gift.
10. Interview the elderly to discover more about their lives.
11. Write to a pen pal in another part of the country.
12. Take classes in CPR and first aid.
13. Take part in an event to raise money for a good cause.
14. Coach a team of younger students.
15. Tutor a younger child who needs special attention.
16. Write appreciation notes to school and community persons.
17. Build birdhouses and place them around the school and community.
18. Organize "litter patrols" for strategic places throughout the school community.
19. Organize a "lost and found" fashion show.
20. Organize a letter-writing and/or telephone campaign to public officials to promote a good cause.
21. Conduct opinion surveys on controversial issues affecting members of your community and publish results in the local newspaper.
22. Attack a school or community problem through a petition drive.
23. Lobby your local legislators for getting a law changed or on the books.
24. Write a proclamation and submit it to your local government asking for a special community recognition day on a topic of your choice such as Environmental Awareness Week or Kindness To Senior Citizens Week.
25. Volunteer to work at a local zoo, museum, humane society, or hospital.

10 Ways To Survive Friday Afternoons, Days Before Spring Breaks, and Other Tense Times

1. Take an ice cream break—teacher's treat! The good will generated will be worth more than the money you spend.

2. Share a favorite joke (one that really makes you laugh), and then ask students to do the same.

3. Call time out for a stretch, stretch and bend, bend and stretch. Teacher leads off, and then allows time for students to take turns as leaders. If classroom conditions allow, use a carefully selected audio- or videotape featuring appropriate background music and movements to spark enthusiasm and lively participation.

4. Set aside a block of time for free reading, a book of choice with no reports due or questions asked. Teacher reads, too!

5. Go for a walk around the school grounds (or the immediate community if school rules permit). Look at and talk about the flora, the fauna, and points of interest you may have missed before—or just walk briskly, breathe deeply, and say goodbye to the stress and boredom that occurs from time to time in even the best and brightest classrooms.

6. Plan and carry out a cooperative learning project with a high-interest content focus. Include time and space for interactive projects, freedom of movement, experimentation, and exploration. In other words, expect pre-planning, discussion, argument, debate, mild frustration, re-planning, more ardent discussion, and, finally, culmination and evaluation leading to a degree of harmony and satisfaction in project completion. A great time should be had by all, and some incidental as well as planned learning is sure to occur.

7. Enjoy a scrap art project! Provide a wide variety of throw-away materials (as many as you can scrounge up from whatever sources available: nuts, bolts, and screws; paper scraps, newspapers and magazines; beads, baubles, and buttons; plastic, metal, and paper container tops; string, yarn, braid, ribbon, and brick-a-brack; fabric, lace, wood, and leather scraps, etc.). Supplement these finds with construction paper, posterboard, glue, paints, crayons, and chalk (as available), and challenge each student to create a masterpiece of his or her own design. Completed projects may range from murals and collages to dioramas and sculptures. The emphasis, of course, will be on the creative process, not the end result.

8. Even though they say it sounds boring, young adolescents never seem to tire of thinking about and talking about "what they like best and what they like least" about school. Ask kids to work in groups to develop a "gripe list" about school rules, regulations, policies, and expectations, followed by a list of suggestions for changes that would help to solve the problems on the "gripe list." Allow time for general group discussion and enjoy the "good old town meeting" glow that comes from hearing the sound of one's voice in open discussion.

9. All work and no play makes Jack, the other students, and the teacher dull boys and girls. Ask students to bring their favorite games to the classroom, add some of your own if you have them, and clear the table for game time. A good "trade off" might be an agreement between students and teachers to work extra hard the first half of the period or to take some extra work home in exchange for additional game time.

10. Play Fruit Basket Turnover! Abandon seating charts, alphabetical order, or other forms of teacher-directed seating, and allow students to rearrange the classroom to better meet personal interests. First establish some ground rules to ensure all students' rights (such as: students may rearrange desks only when the exchange is acceptable to the other person whose desk is being exchanged, is acceptable to the new neighbors, and is not inhibiting to the total group synergy, etc.). Limit the time set aside for moving and build in simple evaluative criteria to determine the duration of the arrangement. The sense of student empowerment afforded by a move of this nature is almost sure to result in improved self-control and classroom management.

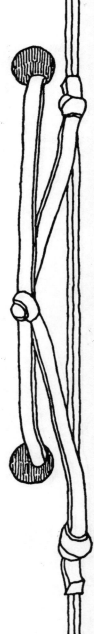

SEPTEMBER

NATIONAL LIBRARY CARD SIGN-UP MONTH

Poll your classmates to see how many have library cards.	Compare a library card with a driver's license.	Invite a public librarian to speak to your class.	Make believe you were accidentally locked in a library by yourself all night. What would you do?	Stretch your imagination and decide how a library is like each of the following: a trip in a time machine, a good movie, a museum, a summer day, and a wonderful dream.
Describe your favorite part of the library. Name ten things that can be found there.	Infer the meaning of this statement: His face is like an open book.	Select a favorite book. Dress and act like a character in the book. See if your classmates can guess your character.	Invent a new way to organize a library.	List three things about which you are very curious to learn more.
Imagine what the world would be like if there were no libraries.	Rewrite a favorite story as a picture book.	About whom would you like to see a book written?	Make a list of your ten favorite books.	Offer suggestions on ways to improve your school's library/media center.
Respond to this statement: Read a good book before Hollywood ruins it.	Describe the people who would use a CONTRA-DICTIONARY.	Pretend you are writing The Great American Novel. What is its title?	Think of three book titles that best describe you.	Which would you rather be: an author, librarian, illustrator, publisher, bookstore owner, book reader, subject of a book, researcher, or editor? Why?

GREAT AMERICAN NOVEL

MYSTERY

AUTOBIOGRAPHY

HOLIDAY ARTS & CRAFTS ✸ ✸

Dancing

COWBOYS OF AMERICA

PETS

ANIMALS

OCTOBER
UNITED NATIONS DAY

Design a new United Nations logo.	What are some ways you can free a country without war and conflict?	Infer the reason the colors of the United Nations' flag are white and blue.	How is the United Nations like the United States? the Olympic Committee? the European Economic Community? the Red Cross?	Diagram the structure of the United Nations. Explain the structure of each branch.
Respond to this statement: The world is getting smaller every day.	Write a story about how two hostile countries resolve their conflicts.	Describe what life today would be like for a person your age in a specific foreign country.	Think of many possible questions, each of which has the word UNITED in its answer.	In what ways would the world be different if we were celebrating UNITED WORLD DAY?
Which countries would you put on a list of "disunited nations"?	Imagine how one person can help keep peace in the world.	Create a timeline of the history of the United Nations.	Explain what the United Nations does and why it is necessary to have such an organization.	Make believe you are a member of the Peace Corps. Where would you like to go? What would you like to do?
If you could interview the President of the United Nations, what would you ask?	Learn how to count to ten in three different languages. Predict when such knowledge might come in handy.	Create a collage of people to celebrate United Nations Day.	Introduce a problem for the "representatives" of a student "United Nations" to solve using the United Nations Charter as a guide.	Respond to this statement: Think globally, act locally.

56

NOVEMBER
VETERANS DAY

Discover why Veterans Day is important to remember and celebrate.	Draw a picture of a medal that a veteran might receive for serving his or her country.	Memorize a song that represents a branch of the military (e.g., "Anchors Aweigh").	Design a new statue/memorial to honor veterans in your community.	What might an American Flag say to a veteran, a Red Cross volunteer, a recruit, a draft dodger, a small child, a new immigrant, and you?
Respond to this statement: Some people wave the American flag but waive what it stands for.	Do you feel more red, white, or blue?	Write a new patriotic song.	Draw a contemporary recruitment poster for the armed forces.	Determine which is more important: peace or security. Give reasons for your answer.
How would life be different if we only retained memories for five years?	Expand on this statement: War is hell.	If you could be bold and brave for a day, what would you do?	List five adjectives that describe your feelings about America.	Debate the issues associated with the presence of women in the military.
What unknown person would you most like to nominate as a great American hero? Why?	If you were a military weapon, what would you say to the soldier who was using you?	Draw a picture of a soldier from any war, wearing the appropriate uniform for the time.	If the men and women remembered on the Vietnam Memorial could speak, what might they say to us as a nation?	With a group of classmates, brainstorm a list of unique ways to solve differences other than waging war. Share your results.

DECEMBER

HUMAN RIGHTS DAY

List all the rights you can think of that are guaranteed by the United States Constitution.	Describe what it means to be a member of a democratic society.	Express what the phrase "human rights" means to you.	If you could improve a human rights issue with a snap of your fingers, what would it be and why?	What truths do you "hold to be self-evident"?
Imagine a world in which all people are permitted basic human rights. Describe this world.	Do species other than the human species have rights? How are those rights denied?	Write to a human rights organization to receive information on what this organization does.	Make believe you have just been given freedom after years of oppression. How do you feel?	Share a newspaper article that reports a violation of human rights.
Define "prejudice." How might prejudice be involved in the denial of someone's human rights?	Investigate the life of immigrant children before child labor laws were put into effect. What are the ten most important facts you have learned?	Show a videotape of Martin Luther King, Jr.'s "I Have A Dream" speech, or read a copy of the speech. Discuss it with classmates.	Elaborate on this thought: Freedom is a package deal.	Identify major human rights issues in our country right now. Compare them to similar issues around the world.
Discover what the 20th Amendment did for human rights in America.	Formulate ten questions to ask persons from a foreign country to find out about the rights they have or don't have in their homeland.	Design a human rights poster to display in school depicting injustices all around the world.	Assemble a list of rules that protect our human rights.	If you could add an eleventh bill to the Bill of Rights, what would it be and why?

58

JANUARY

MARTIN LUTHER KING, JR.'S, BIRTHDAY

What qualities are important in a leader?	Think of six adjectives that most accurately describe Martin Luther King, Jr.	If you had a dream that would make the world a better place, what would it be?	Define civil rights in your own words and discuss with your classmates how civil rights are important to our way of life.	What responsibilities do leaders have?
Identify five positive things Martin Luther King, Jr., did for the people of the United States.	If you could have any leadership role, what would it be and why?	Identify other people who have stood up for what they believed and made a difference.	What did Dr. King do to win the Nobel Peace Prize?	Evaluate the work done by Dr. King's wife and children since his death to continue his dream. Discuss your findings with your classmates.
Why do you think the United States celebrates Martin Luther King, Jr.'s birthday?	Think of a civil rights issue and create a slogan or song that is catchy.	Create a timeline that displays the major events and accomplishments in Dr. King's life.	Design a civil rights poster.	Respond to this statement: Education can't make us all leaders—but it can teach us which leader to follow.
If you were alive during Dr. King's lifetime, would you have participated in the March on Washington? Why or why not?	Create an abstract picture using colors which represent freedom and equal rights.	What qualities do good leaders possess?	Compile a list of all major civil rights laws passed by Congress, starting with the Bill of Rights. Rank order them by personal importance to you.	Define these terms: boycott, equality, discrimination, rally, and prohibit.

FEBRUARY

FREEDOM DAY

Decide which is more important to you: freedom of speech, or freedom of religion. Defend your answer.	What are all the "free" words you can think of?	Learn a few songs from American history that can be associated with freedom. Sing one for the class.	Organize a Freedom Day celebration in your class, including a contest for best-dressed freedom fighter.	Discuss with your classmates the struggles of one modern-day country as it attempts to gain freedom from oppressive rule; bring in newspaper articles depicting this struggle.
Which colors best represent freedom? Why do you think so?	Construct a flag of the United States using paper chains.	Respond to the slogan "America, Land of the Free."	Identify all the rules you must follow in your school; then list all the freedoms you have next to each.	Design a monument to soldiers in the American Revolution.
Brainstorm some terms, events, or feelings that remind you of freedom.	If you had a freedom treasure chest, what would be inside?	Define the word "freedom" in your own words. Give examples of the freedoms you enjoy.	What does it mean to "let freedom ring"?	Does freedom feel more like a flag or a rainbow? a poem or a song? a parade or a ball game? New Year's Day or the Fourth of July?
Explain the statement: "It's a free country." Which new countries can make this claim since 1990?	Why do you think the American Revolutionaries thought freedom was so important?	If you were free to do whatever you wished for one whole day, what would you do?	Present to your class the story of a famous freedom fighter from American history.	Choose a person or persons to receive a special freedom award. Explain your choice(s). Design the award you would present.

FREEDOM DAY

MARCH
WOMEN IN HISTORY MONTH

Draw a picture describing how a famous woman influenced America. Identify the woman.	Ask a grandparent how women's roles have changed since he or she was your age.	Report on a famous woman in history.	Consider why you feel there have been no female presidents in our country though there have been female heads of state in many other countries.	Debate in class the question of whether women should be allowed all the privileges men currently have.
List as many famous women as you can who are not from the United States.	Debate this statement: Women make better teachers than do men.	Create a timeline depicting all major accomplishments in the fight for women's rights.	List some occupations which have been traditionally held by males but in which women have recently made great strides.	Discover a local female who has reached a level of achievement previously reserved for males. Invite her to address your class.
If you were a TV talk show host, what woman would you want to interview today? Why?	Make believe you have done something that would earn you a place in the history books. What did you do?	Research the Equal Rights Amendment and decide whether you are for or against its passage.	Design a unit of currency with the face of a famous woman.	In your opinion, what obstacles still deter women from achieving the same goals as men? Explain.
What challenges do women of the 90s face?	Read an article that pertains to a woman's issue and summarize it for the class.	Name ten famous women and list one accomplishment of each.	Ask several people to nominate a "Woman of the Year." Find out why each chose the person he or she did.	Of the following people, which one has traits that you admire the most? Calamity Jane, Jackie Kennedy Onassis, Coretta Scott King, Betsy Ross, Pocahontas, Margaret Thatcher, or Hillary Clinton?

Calamity Jane

Pocahontas
(Lady Rebecca)

Harriette
Tubman

APRIL

EARTH DAY

When we say, "It is raining," what do we mean by "it"?	Rename the Earth to better describe its qualities.	How might "progress" mean different things to different people?	Discover the role that the Environmental Protection Agency plays in our government.	Present a school forum or debate on environmental issues.
Discover why our planet is called "Mother Earth."	Why is the sky blue?	Explain the importance of conservation.	Organize a recycling program for your school cafeteria.	How can the following items help save the Earth? Bicycle, baking soda, cloth diaper, seeding, compost pile, power switch.
Compose a song for Earth Day that explains the importance of preserving the Earth.	The Earth is the answer. What is the question?	Research and write about the depletion of the ozone layer.	Design an Earth Day poster.	What is your most important environmental belief?
Decide whether you are more like a flashlight or a candle. Explain.	List all the words you can think of that begin with the word "earth" (e.g., earthworm).	Explain all the different ways a tree influences our lives.	Organize a cleanup effort for your school campus or a local park.	Would you rather be a rainbow or a moonbeam?

EARTH DAY

62

MAY

MEMORIAL DAY

Research one conflict/war that has occurred in the 20th century. Briefly summarize your findings on one page.	History is to a nation what memory is to an individual. What do you think this means?	Discover the origin of Memorial Day and why we celebrate it.	Share what you did during the Memorial Day weekend.	Attendance at Memorial Day parades has declined over the past few years. Why do you think this has happened?
Design a new flag for our country that would represent the attitude of Americans during the 20th century.	Determine what you think "America, the beautiful" means.	Respond to this statement: Memory is a wonderful treasure chest for those who know how to pack it.	Explain an emotion you have had at a memorial service or a patriotic parade.	Examine the concept of patriotism and consider its role in a nation's success.
Decide what you want your tombstone to say when you die.	Of all the local, state, or national memorials with which you are familiar, which one is your favorite?	Plan an ideal Memorial Day celebration for your community.	If it could speak to your family, what might the statue of Lincoln in the Lincoln Memorial say?	For what great deed or special accomplishment would you most like to be remembered?
Select a personal hero; design a memorial to him or her.	If you could ask Norman Schwartzkopf one question, what would you ask? Why?	Draw a poster honoring our nation's armed services.	Consider whether our national anthem should be changed. If so, to what song?	Respond to this statement: Today there are no heroes for kids to look up to.

JUNE
END OF SCHOOL/SUMMER VACATION

If you had the money to do anything or go anywhere you wanted during summer vacation, where would you go and with whom would you like to go?	What if you could see an old friend you haven't seen for a long time? Which friend would you pick and what would you do?	Compare summer vacation to the winter holidays.	Construct a summer collage.	Write a thank-you note to your teacher for his or her assistance this school year.
Acquire souvenirs from activities this summer and show them to your new class in the fall.	Outline your idea of the perfect summer day.	If you had to choose one or the other, would you rather be without heat in the winter or without air-conditioning in the summer? Why?	List the ten best things about summer vacation.	Set ten goals for yourself which you hope to accomplish over the summer.
Be honest. Do you ever miss school during summer vacation? Explain.	Write a letter to yourself explaining what you will do this summer. In the fall, compare this letter to the actual events that took place.	If summer vacation requires that parents go to school, describe the students your parents would become.	If you could spend the summer with a family from another culture, where would you like to go and why?	Write a haiku about the summer.
Act out your favorite summer activity for the class.	Describe summer to a person who lives at the North Pole.	Design a word puzzle using words associated with summer vacation.	When does a minute seem like an hour? When does an hour seem like a minute?	Design a summer vacation poster or travel brochure.

USING A VARIETY OF STRATEGIES TO DIFFERENTIATE INSTRUCTION

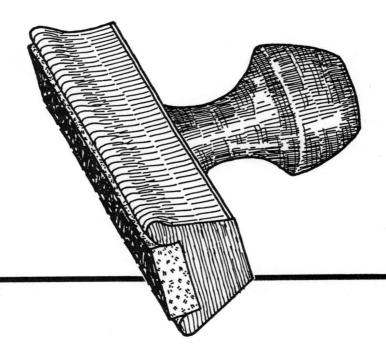

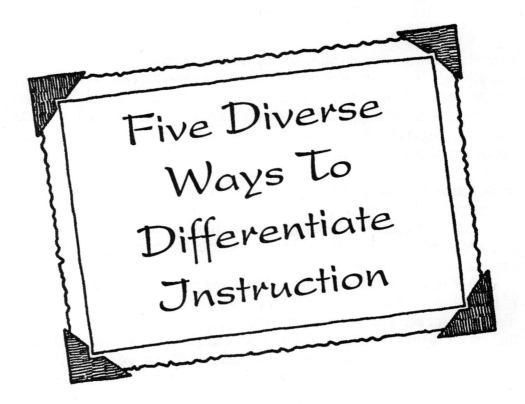

Five Diverse Ways To Differentiate Instruction

On the following pages, you will find five diverse ways to differentiate instruction in the classroom. These reproducible materials may be used with individual students or with small groups of students.

Pocket Packet Format: *Hot-Air Balloons*

This is a set of task cards designed around a theme and made to be stored in a 5" x 8" manila envelope. These materials are particularly appealing if colored (by students) and laminated and may be especially useful as part of a learning center program or for students who finish classwork early. See pages 69–71.

File Folder Format: *Optical Illusions*

This activity, pages 72–74, is to be mounted on a regular size file folder. There is a cover sheet to be colored (by students) and mounted on the front of the file folder for easy storage. These are good activities for independent use and are useful in a learning center program. For answer key, see page 303.

Portable Desk Top Format: *Collage of Feelings*

This set of materials, pages 75–79, is to be colored, cut out, and pasted on a three-sided display board. These boards can be cut from a medium-sized cardboard box or purchased through a local office supply store.

Learning Center Format: *Leading into Language*

The term "learning center" is used to designate a physical area where students engage in a variety of learning activities and experiences. The character and design of a learning center is determined by the center's theme, concepts, and skills to be taught or reinforced and the students' interests and abilities. A learning center must offer choices and alternatives in order to involve students in a very personal manner in the total learning experience. An unidisciplinary center includes experiences and activities confined to the teaching of one or more specific concepts related to one specific content area. A multidisciplinary center offers experiences and activities related to one topic but provides for the integration of several content areas and skills levels. Leading into Language, pages 80–86, is a multidisciplinary learning center. It is designed to reinforce the use of communication skills for students working at three distinctly different levels.

Task Cards for Independent Study: *Reference Referral*

Independent study projects allow students to work at their own rates and in keeping with their own learning styles. Higher-level thinking skills are best developed in an atmosphere of freedom from undue pressure generated by competition with peers and the ever-present struggle to "finish on time."

One effective strategy for independent study is the task card approach in which a series of sequentially organized task cards is presented to the student with clearly written directions for completion, an agreed-upon time plan, a culminating project, and a specific and clearly defined plan for evaluation. See sample Task-by-Task Independent Study Project (including task cards ready to be reproduced, cut apart, and pasted on index cards for immediate use by students), pages 87–89, and sample outline, page 90.

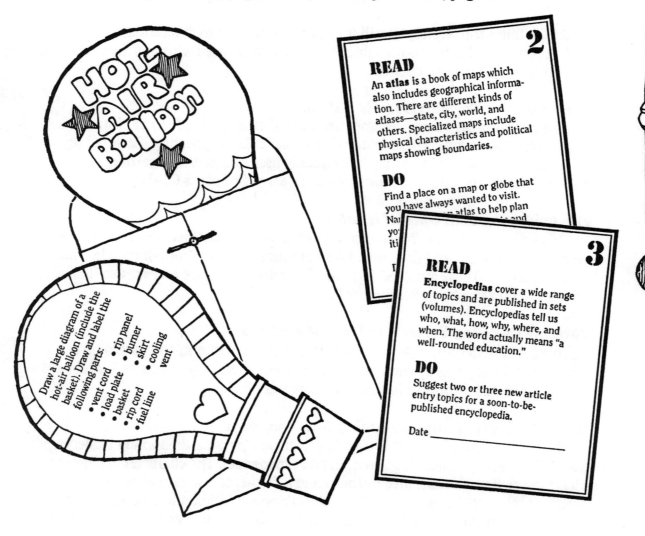

HOT-AIR Balloon

Draw a large diagram of a hot-air balloon (include the basket). Draw and label the following parts:
• vent cord • rip panel
• load plate • burner
• basket • skirt
• rip cord • cooling
• fuel line vent

2

READ

An **atlas** is a book of maps which also includes geographical information. There are different kinds of atlases—state, city, world, and others. Specialized maps include physical characteristics and political maps showing boundaries.

DO

Find a place on a map or globe that you have always wanted to visit. Na͟ atlas to help plan
yo͟
iti

3

READ

Encyclopedias cover a wide range of topics and are published in sets (volumes). Encyclopedias tell us who, what, how, why, where, and when. The word actually means "a well-rounded education."

DO

Suggest two or three new article entry topics for a soon-to-be-published encyclopedia.

Date _____

POCKET PACKET TASK CARDS

Hot-Air Balloon

Draw a large diagram of a hot-air balloon (include the basket). Draw and label the following parts:

- vent cord
- load plate
- basket
- rip cord
- fuel line
- rip panel
- burner
- skirt
- cooling vent

Design your own hot-air balloon to reflect your personality.

Hot Air Balloon

POCKET PACKET TASK CARDS

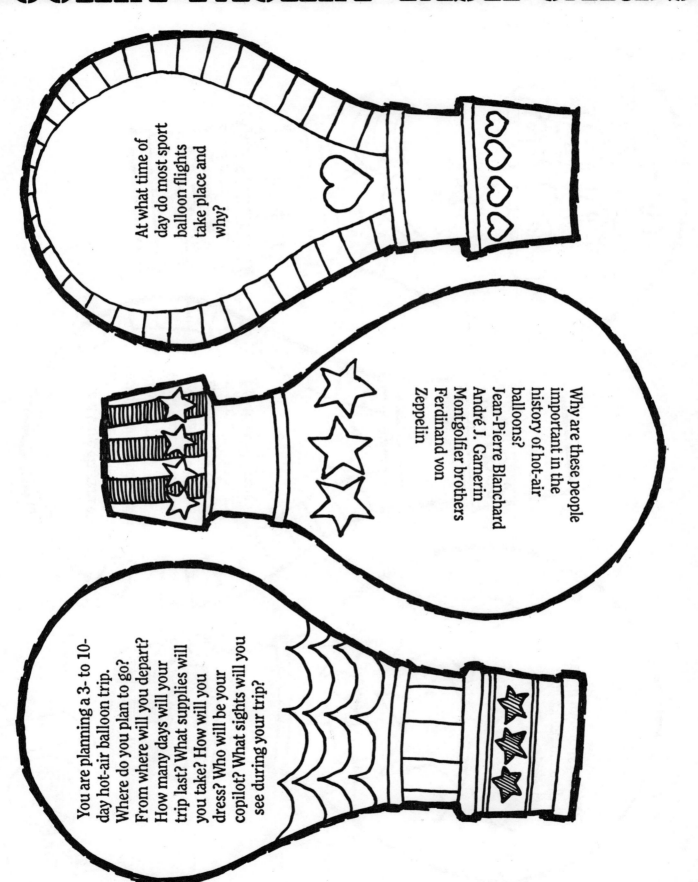

At what time of day do most sport balloon flights take place and why?

Why are these people important in the history of hot-air balloons?
Jean-Pierre Blanchard
André J. Garnerin
Montgolfier brothers
Ferdinand von Zeppelin

You are planning a 3- to 10-day hot-air balloon trip. Where do you plan to go? From where will you depart? How many days will your trip last? What supplies will you take? How will you dress? Who will be your copilot? What sights will you see during your trip?

POCKET PACKET TASK CARDS

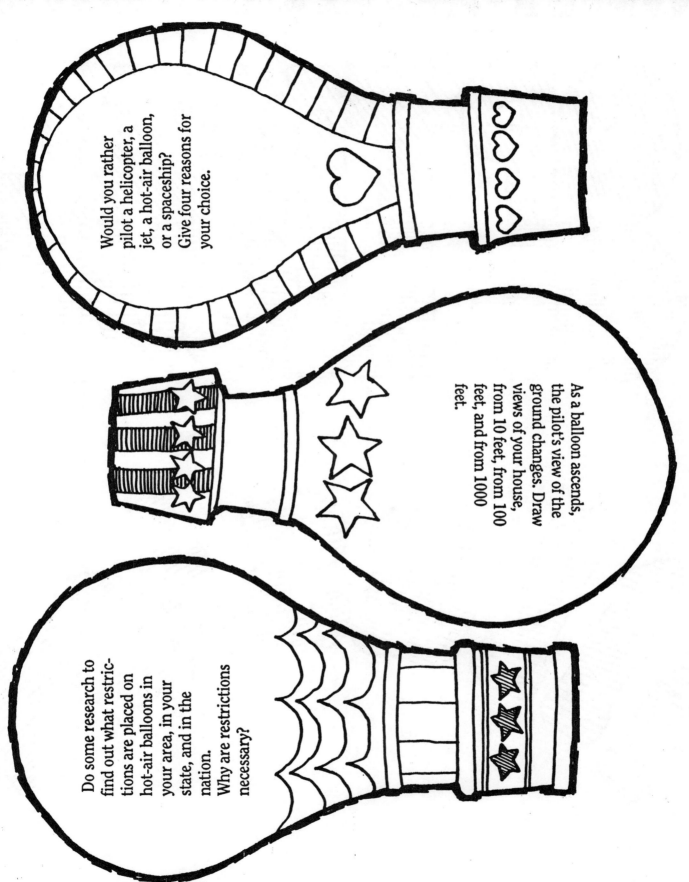

Would you rather pilot a helicopter, a jet, a hot-air balloon, or a spaceship? Give four reasons for your choice.

As a balloon ascends, the pilot's view of the ground changes. Draw views of your house, from 10 feet, from 100 feet, and from 1000 feet.

Do some research to find out what restrictions are placed on hot-air balloons in your area, in your state, and in the nation. Why are restrictions necessary?

OPTICAL ILLUSION

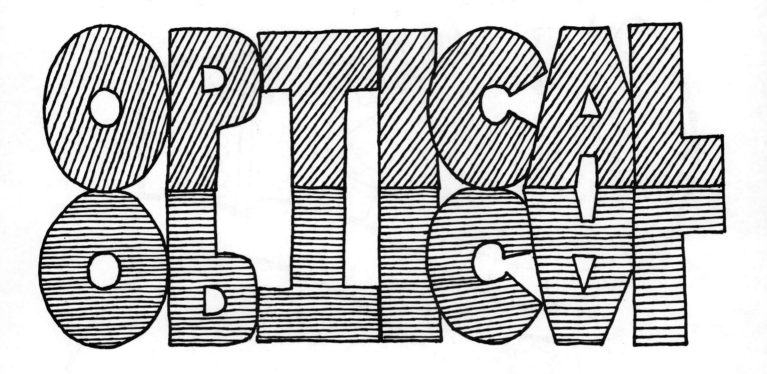

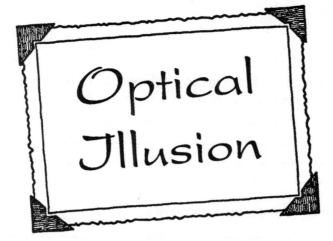

Optical Illusion

OBJECTIVES

. . . You will know the meaning of the term "optical illusion."

. . . You will understand some of the different things that cause optical illusions.

. . . You will begin to observe optical illusions in the world around you.

QUESTIONS

1. What does the word optical mean? _____

_____

_____

What does the word illusion mean? _____

_____

_____

Therefore, what do you think an optical illusion is? _____

_____

_____

_____

_____

2. Reversible images are a type of optical illusion. Look at this series of vases long enough, and what do you begin to see?

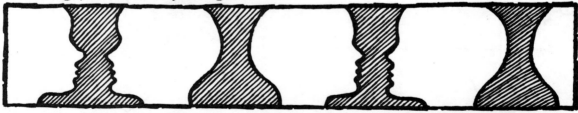

3. Because of the way the eye works, the image on the retina depends on **angular** size rather than **actual** size.

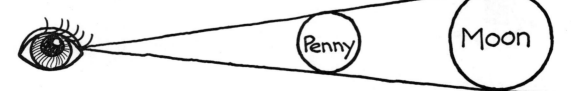

The crossing lines may form a narrow angle and a small image, or a wide angle and a large image. However, the size of an angle depends not only on the size of the object, but on its distance from the observer. Therefore, how can a penny held in front of the eye block out the much larger moon in the night sky? _____

_____

_____

_____

4. What is the meaning of the word perspective? _____

_____

_____

5. Three drawings of the same cube are shown below. Because of differences in perspective, they look like three completely different shapes. Can you see the cube in each drawing?

6. Position and distance also play a role in how we perceive things. Look at each of the figures below and tell a.) how they seem to compare in size by simply looking at them and b.) how they actually compare in size, discovered by tracing one part and placing the tracing over the other part.

Example:

a) X looks longer than Y
b) X and y are equal

①

a) _____
b) _____

②

a) _____
b) _____

③

a) _____
b) _____

④

a) _____
b) _____

Name _____

Portable Desktop Center

PURPOSE
An interactive portable desktop center in which students make a collage of their feelings.

SETTING UP
Use the patterns and examples provided to arrange a portable desktop learning center. Patterns may be enlarged, reduced, colored, or used as they are.

HOW TO USE
Color and arrange all patterns on a three-sided display board. Add a pocket to each flower pattern. Duplicate enough copies of the collage pieces for the entire class. Cut apart and separate into groups. Store these pieces in the flower pockets. Each student takes a pattern (collage piece) to complete. When students have finished all eight patterns, they use them to create a collage poster of their feelings.

WHAT TO DO . . .

Make a collage of your feelings:

Take a small flower from each of the larger flowers displayed on this "Collage of Feelings" three-sided board. Write a response to each.

Once you have completed all eight, creatively arrange your flowers on a poster. Add other information such as:

- your name.
- a title.
- words to describe you.

Have fun!

76

WHAT TO DO...

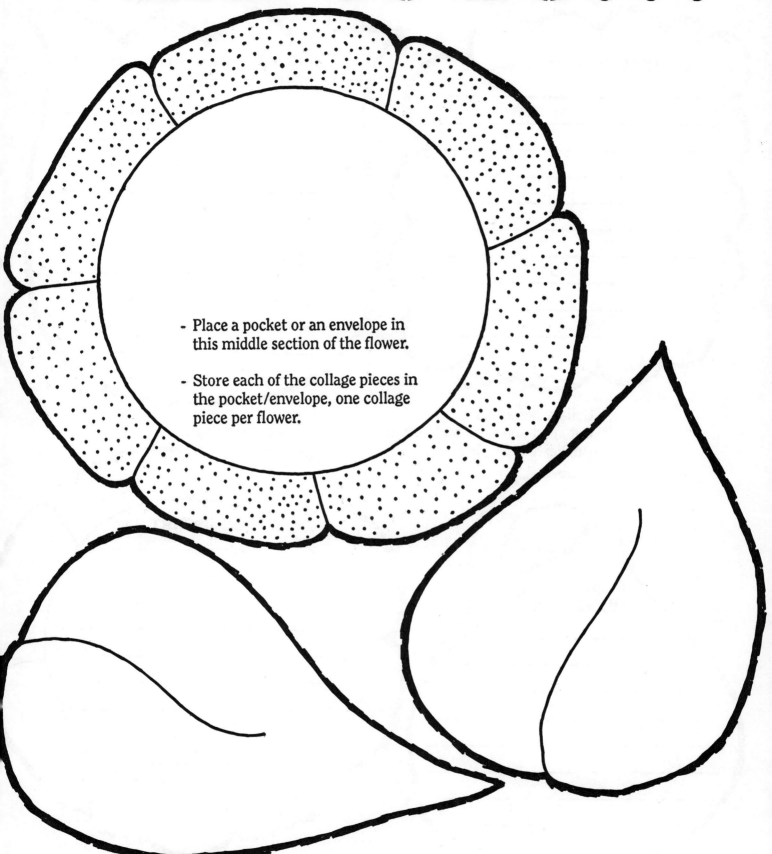

- Place a pocket or an envelope in this middle section of the flower.

- Store each of the collage pieces in the pocket/envelope, one collage piece per flower.

WHAT TO DO...

It's like a **THORN** in my side when _____
_____
_____
_____
_____
_____
_____
_____
_____

In the **GARDEN** of life, the most important ingredients to me are _____
_____
_____
_____
_____
_____
_____
_____
_____
_____
_____

Collage pieces . . .
Cut apart and store each one in a separate pocket or envelope.
Duplicate multiple copies.

People say I **BLOSSOM** when
_____
_____
_____
_____
_____

I feel like **DIRT** after
_____
_____
_____
_____
_____
_____

WHAT TO DO . . .

The time I **ROSE** to my highest pinnacle allowed me to _____
_____
_____
_____
_____
_____
_____
_____
_____

The best time to **LEAVE** me alone is _____
_____
_____
_____
_____
_____
_____
_____
_____
_____
_____
_____
_____

Collage pieces . . .
Cut apart and store each one in a separate pocket or envelope.
Duplicate multiple copies.

I really **DIG**
_____
_____
_____
_____
_____
_____

To make me
SPRING into action,
just
_____
_____
_____
_____
_____
_____

Learning Center Format: Leading Into Language

CONTENT AREA: Language Arts

SKILLS: Critical Reading
Vocabulary Enrichment
Word Usage
Creative Writing

Note: This plan is for a large center with a distinct area designated for each skill. Sitting/writing space should be provided for at least 8 to 10 students.

CRITICAL READING

I. Objectives
- A. Central Purpose: Students should be able to recognize and interpret hidden "intent" or "inference" in written communication.
- B. Specific Purposes:
  - *Level I:* Students can recognize and isolate words intended to create emotional appeal.
  - *Level II:* Students can associate recognized intentions and inferences with the human needs and emotions to which they appeal and are able to create like appeals through written communication.
  - *Level III:* Students are able to make personal judgments about the worth and morality of attempts to deceive through the medium of public advertising.

II. Tools and Materials
Four or five large, attractive magazine ads, mounted and displayed on a bulletin board or protected in acetate sheets and placed in a box or envelope; paper, pencils, scissor, paste, plain and colored construction paper; large, empty board space where students can display original ads.

III. Operational Procedure
- A. Introduction of Center Area and Directions for Use:
  1. Discuss general purpose and use of advertising; go over all instructions.
  2. Point out art supplies and empty board space for original displays.
  3. Ask students to make suggestions about how original ads may be used for evaluative purposes. Schedule a future time to make a final decision related to this.

Learning Center Format: Leading Into Language

B. Procedures:

Level I: Ask student to choose *words* from the ads that make the reader "want to buy" and list them on paper.

OR

Student may write a sentence about each ad, telling how it makes him or her *feel*.

Optional: Student may design own ad for an imaginary product, place it on the board, and see how many "buyers" the ad attracts.

Evaluation: Written work; optional work, group decision.

Level II: Ask student to read ads and make a list of the human emotions or needs to which they appeal.

OR

Student may make up three ads of his or her own which use the same psychology or emotional appeal as three of the displayed ads.

Optional: Same as *Level I*

Evaluation: Written work; optional work, group decision.

Level III: Ask student to read ads and write a sentence explaining real intent of each ad.

AND/OR

Take a position: "With which of the following statements do you agree? Write a paragraph to explain your choice."

1. Advertisers should be required by law to be totally honest; they should not be permitted to use subtle deceit to sell products to the general public.
2. America is a "free-press" society. Advertisers ought to be allowed to print anything they wish; if the public is deceived, it is its own fault for not buying cautiously.

Optional: Same as *Level I.*

Evaluation: Written work; optional, group decision.

Learning Center Format: Leading Into Language

VOCABULARY ENRICHMENT

I. Objectives
A. Central Purpose: Students should be able to use descriptive words with increasing sensitivity and precision.

B. Specific Purposes:

Levels I and II: Students can demonstrate sensitivity and precision in the use of adjectives by matching descriptive words with the real-life situations they *best* describe.

Level III: Students can demonstrate skill in making word associations and drawing inferences by choosing from many possible life situations the one *best* described by each of ten sentences.

II. Tools and Materials
Six or seven large, colorful pictures demonstrating human emotion (numbered 1 through 7); bulletin board space or substitute; pencil, paper, 3" x 5" cards, tacks or tape; six or seven envelopes—one attached behind or below each picture . . .

Level I: 10 to 12 word cards bearing adjectives which can be associated with chosen pictures—i.e., *angry, sad, embarrassed, disgusted, overjoyed, anxious, impatient, excited,* etc.

Level II: 10 to 12 word cards—same as *Level I* with more difficult words (i.e., *furious, harassed, exuberant, amorous, exhilarated, implacable, arrogant,* etc.)

Level III: 10 to 15 cards bearing sentences which describe, by inference, the emotions displayed by the pictures (i.e., *"Serious consequences follow infraction of rules." "Feelings are not often camouflaged by facial expression." "Ingenious minds excel in clever design."*)

III. Operational Procedure
A. Introduction of Center Area and Directions for Use:
1. Locate all materials and demonstrate use of word and sentence cards.
2. Give directions for adding cards to envelopes.
3. Ask students to think, as they work at the center, about ways in which the envelopes of collected word cards might be used to evaluate skills in precision of word choice and in word sensitivity. Set a future time for making suggestions.

Learning Center Format: Leading Into Language

B. Procedures:

Level I: Ask student to match each Level I word card with the mounted picture it *best* describes and explain his or her choices to a friend.

OR

Student may number the pictures on paper and list the words matched with each picture; discuss choices with friend or teacher.

Required: Student must, on a 3" x 5" card, write an additional word of his or her own for each picture and insert it in the envelope below each corresponding picture.

Level II: Same as *Level I,* substituting *Level II* word cards.

Level III: Same as *Level I* and *II,* substituting *Level III* sentence cards.

Evaluation—All Levels: Group decision

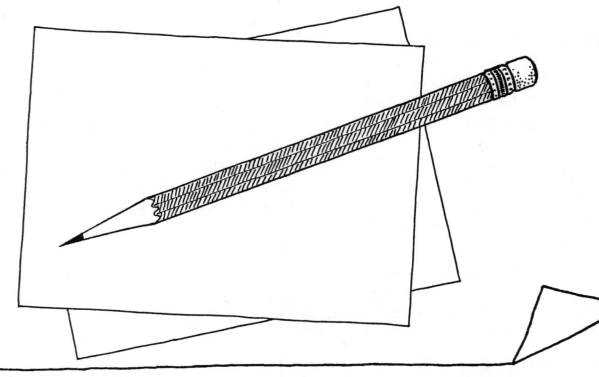

Learning Center Format: Leading Into Language

WORD USAGE

I. Objectives

A. General Objective: Students should be able to recognize and classify words according to their uses in the context of a sentence.

B. Specific Objectives:

Level I: Students can recognize and use verbs and adjectives in context.

Levels II and III: Students can recognize and classify nouns, verbs, adjectives, and adverbs according to their uses in context.

II. Tools and Materials

Level I: Duplicated sheets of a list of ten simple nouns.

Levels II and III: Duplicated sheets bearing the following paragraph:

Horskly, the minkled gooks kittled. The murks skorked the grunches and rittled the morks. The runches gloored skatily, and the grimped gottles griffled. The make mootled mortily.

All: Pencils, crayons, paper.

III. Operational Procedure

A. Introduction of Center Area and Directions for Use:

1. Define *noun, verb, adjective, adverb* and discuss examples of each with group.
2. Identify materials and read all directions; answer any questions.

B. Procedures:

Level I: Ask student to locate the duplicated list of ten nouns. *Before* each noun, student will write a descriptive word that makes sense. *After* each noun, student will add an action word that makes sense. Then he or she should read each phrase silently.

OR

Student may write three original sentences, each containing a noun, verb, and adjective. He or she may classify the words by *circling* all verbs and *underlining* all adjectives.

Evaluation: Written work—number of words used or classified properly.

Learning Center Format: Leading Into Language

Level II: Ask student to obtain duplicated nonsense story. He or she must classify all nouns, verbs, adjectives, and adverbs by using a color code of his or her own. (Remind student to add a color key, so that the classification may be understood.)

OR

Student may write five original sentences, using *real* words, and classify all four kinds of words by listing them under the headings NOUN—VERB—ADJECTIVE—ADVERB at the bottom of the paper.

Evaluation: Written work—number of words properly classified.

Level III: Same as *Level II*

OR

Student may compose original story of nonsense words and classify nouns, verbs, adjectives, and adverbs by any method student chooses to devise.

Evaluation: Written work—number of words properly classified.

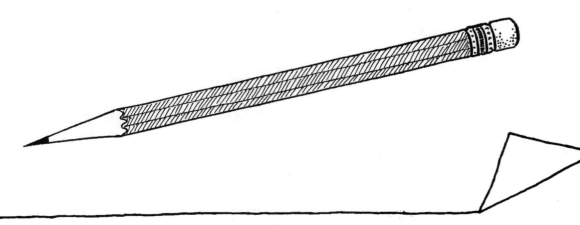

Learning Center Format: Leading Into Language

CREATIVE WRITING

I. Objectives
A. General Objective: Student will be able to demonstrate skills in association, transference, and writing style by translating, either from reading or memory, a fable or folktale into a present-day journalistic-style news or feature story.

II. Tools and Materials
An abbreviated form of the story "Rip Van Winkle" and a model report of that story as it might appear in the news or feature section of a local newspaper if "Rip" had been discovered just this week. Duplicated copies of a similar folktale, paper, pencil; duplicating masters (optional).

III. Operational Procedure
A. Introduction of Center and Directions for Use:

1. Identify materials, review directions.

2. Discuss "journalistic" style—as compared with ordinary prose. Mention the key words *Who—What—When—Where—Why* and add *items of human and public interest* (and *opinion,* in feature stories).

3. Discuss how the *optional* activity might be best accomplished. Set a time for those who choose that activity to make final decisions.

B. Procedures:

All Levels: Ask student to read abbreviated story of "Rip Van Winkle" and its corresponding model of a modern-day news or feature story.
Ask him or her then to read a second similar story, chosen by the teacher, and to write a corresponding modern-day news or feature account of the story in journalistic style.

OR

Student may do the same assignment using a folktale of his or her own choosing.

Optional: Any student may submit his or her story for publication in a local class newspaper. The process of collecting, preparing, and duplicating the paper will be determined by a committee of those electing to participate.

Reference Referral:
A Task-by-Task Independent Study Project

Title: REFERENCE REFERRAL

Date To Begin: _____   **Date To Complete:** _____

Dates To Check with My Teacher: _____   _____

_____   _____   _____

Major Objective:
To become familiar with and make use of a variety of reference books and tools in order to become a more creative and critical thinker.

Procedure:
1. Read and relate to each of the task cards in the packet.
2. Discuss the directions for completion with my teacher and ask for help in locating any materials I may not know where to find.
3. Agree upon the dates to check with my teacher and the dates of completion. Make my plan of action.

Tasks and Plan of Action:
See ready-to-reproduce-and-use task cards, pages 88–89.

Culminating Project and Plan of Action:
See Task Card Number 8.

Name _____

Teacher _____

1

1. Read through the card pack carefully—read and relate to each of the task cards in the packet.

2. Discuss the directions for completion with my teacher and ask for help in locating any materials I may not know where to find.

3. Agree upon the dates to check with my teacher and the dates of completion. Make my Plan of Action.

2

READ

An **atlas** is a book of maps which also includes geographical information. There are different kinds of atlases—state, city, world, and others. Specialized maps include physical characteristics and political maps showing boundaries.

DO

Find a place on a map or globe that you have always wanted to visit. Name it. Use an atlas to help plan your trip; explain your route and itinerary.

Date _____

3

READ

Encyclopedias cover a wide range of topics and are published in sets (volumes). Encyclopedias tell us who, what, how, why, where, and when. The word actually means "a well-rounded education."

DO

Suggest two or three new article entry topics for a soon-to-be-published encyclopedia.

Date _____

4

READ

One of the volumes in a set of encyclopedias is the **index**. The index is an alphabetical listing of topics and the many different volumes or pages where information may be found.

DO

Create a series of ten "scavenger hunt" clues which will lead a friend to a specific encyclopedia article.

Date _____

5

READ

A **dictionary** is an alphabetical listing of words which includes syllabification, pronunciation, parts of speech, meanings, usage notes, and etymology.

DO

Imagine that you are the author of a new student slang dictionary. Write ten entries for your new reference tool, following the format of a traditional dictionary for each one.

Date _____

6

READ

Another reference book is called a **thesaurus.** This book is arranged alphabetically and includes synonyms for specific words.

DO

Pretend that "thesaurus" is a name of a creature related to the dinosaur. Draw this creature. Add to its name if you wish.

Date _____

7

READ

Other reference books include: **gazetteer, biographical dictionary,** and **book of quotations.** All include cross references (denoted by **See** or **See also**), which suggest other topics for more information.

DO

Compile an ABCs of Reference Books and Materials for younger students.

Date _____

8

1. Check your completed work and arrange it in your portfolio in sequential order.

2. Share the completed portfolio with your teacher and be prepared to discuss which of the tasks turned out to be your best work. Which tasks were the most difficult for you to complete and which tasks challenged your ability to think critically?

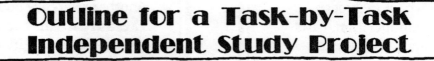

Outline for a Task-by-Task Independent Study Project

Title: _____

Date to Begin: _____ Date to Complete: _____

Dates to Check with My Teacher: _____ _____

_____ _____ _____

Major Objective: _____

_____

_____

Procedure: _____

_____

_____

_____

Tasks and Plan of Action: _____

_____

_____

_____

Culminating Project: _____

_____

_____

Evaluation: _____

_____

_____

_____

_____

_____

Independent Study Checklist

_____ Fits the developmental needs of the student

_____ Is planned to meet a specific student-centered goal

_____ Is only one part of a plan of balanced learning experiences and is integrated into the overall curriculum in a manner that is readily evident to the student

_____ Encourages the use of creative and higher-level thinking skills

_____ The central academic purpose is clearly understood by the student and the procedure for completion is in keeping with the student's learning style, past experiences, and skills

_____ Includes clear, concise instructions which are not dependent on the teacher

_____ Provides for growth in personal research and study skills

_____ Specifies reference and resource materials that are readily available and meaningful to the student

_____ Is presented as attractively and interestingly as possible

_____ Includes introductory and background information and evaluative criteria that are understandable and meaningful to students

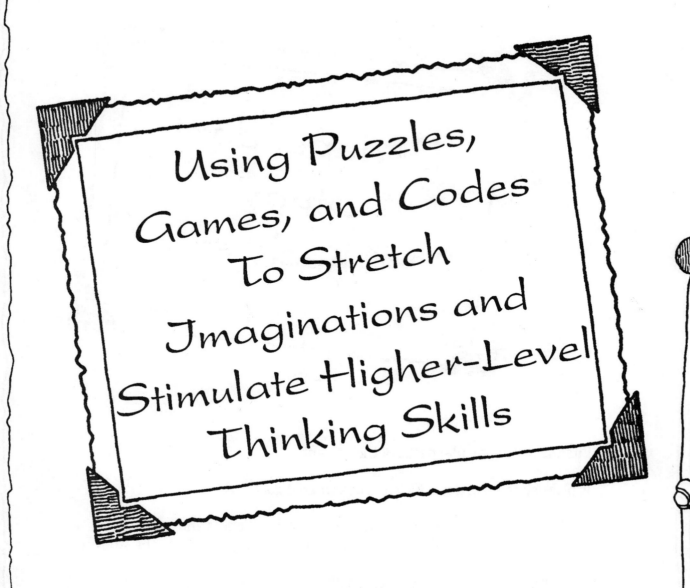

Using Puzzles, Games, and Codes To Stretch Imaginations and Stimulate Higher-Level Thinking Skills

Puzzles, games, and codes can be prepared ahead for use as components of interdisciplinary units to stretch imaginations, sharpen thinking skills, teach or reinforce basic skills and/or concepts, and for "something to do" during that unexpected thirty minutes or so when all of a sudden there's "nothing to do" to stave off boredom and keep those active minds occupied.

Using high-interest themes and an attractive non-threatening format will foster a positive attitude and present the activity as "something done for the students rather than something being done to them." In other words, they will be more apt to view the project as a privilege instead of a chore.

Current events, entertainment and sports figures, space, exotic destinations, math and science challenges, environmentalism, technology, ancient civilizations, and cultural diversity are some topics that might be used as the focus for teacher- and student-made projects.

The game collection might also include some commercial games selected to sharpen logical thinking skills and encourage the development of interpersonal and socialization skills. The following list includes games that are readily available in most game stores and are relatively inexpensive. In some instances, students may be able to bring games from home to share on a temporary basis, or parents might be alerted to look for used games in good condition at yard sales.

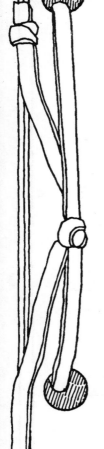

BATTLESHIP by Milton Bradley

BOGGLE by Parker Brothers

BY JOVE by Aristoplay

CLUE by Parker Brothers

MASTER-MIND by Invicta Plastics

PROBE by Parker Brothers

PSYC-OUT by Mag Nif

QUBIC by Parker Brothers

SCRABBLE by Milton Bradley

STOCK MARKET by Avalon Hill

TRIVIAL PURSUIT by Parker Brothers

TUF by Avalon Hill

Puzzles and codes might include crosswords, word-finds, math teasers, visual discrimination, and other formats of unique appeal to your students. Challenge the more creative and ambitious students to develop original works to add to the collection. They will be particularly inspired if you assure them that the best ones will be reproduced and presented to the whole class. (Don't forget to establish criteria to be used when selecting the puzzles; more importantly, don't forget to use all the appropriately developed puzzles in a timely manner.)

On the following pages you will find sample mind-stretchers ready to reproduce and use.

Thinking About Games

Read all of the following questions and think about each one carefully before you begin to write your answers. Use the back of the page if you need more room.

1. Games can help students strengthen their thinking skills by _____
_____
_____
_____

2. My teachers do or do not (circle one) use games that strengthen thinking skills in the classroom because _____
_____
_____
_____

3. Some games that I play outside school that I think help me develop thinking skills are:
_____
_____
_____

4. Playing games with my classmates helps me to learn more about getting along with other people by _____
_____
_____

5. Playing games with my classmates helps me to learn the following things about myself:
_____
_____
_____

6. The game I like best of all is _____
because _____
_____
_____

7. I think computer games are _____
_____

8. Some games I wish we had in our classroom are: _____
_____
_____

Name _____

It's Your Game

Use the gameboard worksheet on page 96 to design a board game to teach or reinforce a variety of skills and/or concepts in one of the suggested content areas on a separate sheet of paper. Provide complete rules and directions for playing your game.

LANGUAGE ARTS
A game based on a well-known novel, fable, or biography.

SOCIAL STUDIES
A game to review ancient civilizations, cultural diversity, or approaches to conflict resolution.

MATH
A game to reinforce the use of consumer math skills, decimals, or money management.

SCIENCE
A game to review geology, ecology, or world geography.

BONUS
Design a set of trivia game questions for a chapter in your social studies or science textbook. Use these questions to review for a class assignment or quiz.

My Project Plan

The title of my project will be: _____

I will begin on (date): _____ I will finish on: _____

Materials I will need from the media center are:

_____

_____

_____

Some problems I might have with this project are: _____

_____

_____

_____

_____

Name _____

START

←

Name _____

Territorially Speaking

A territory is an area of land that is owned or controlled by an independent country. All but nineteen of the fifty United States were once territories. The Philippines became an independent country, while Puerto Rico and the northern Mariana Islands became U.S. commonwealths.

Today there are four main United States territories, each an island or collection of islands. **Guam** and the Virgin Islands are unincorporated territories. Two wholly unorganized and unincorporated territories are American Samoa and the Pacific Islands. All except the Pacific Islands govern themselves and have non-voting representatives in Congress. Two of the **Pacific Islands** are **Wake** and **Midway;** two of the **Virgin Islands** are **St. Croix** and **St. John;** two of the islands of **American Samoa** are **Tutuila** and **Swains.** Find and circle these territories (in bold letters in this paragraph) in the puzzle below. Remember, there are four main territories. Their names read from left to right. Look a little harder, and you will find the names of some of the islands that make up these territories. These names read from top to bottom and each one intersects the name of the territory of which it is a part.

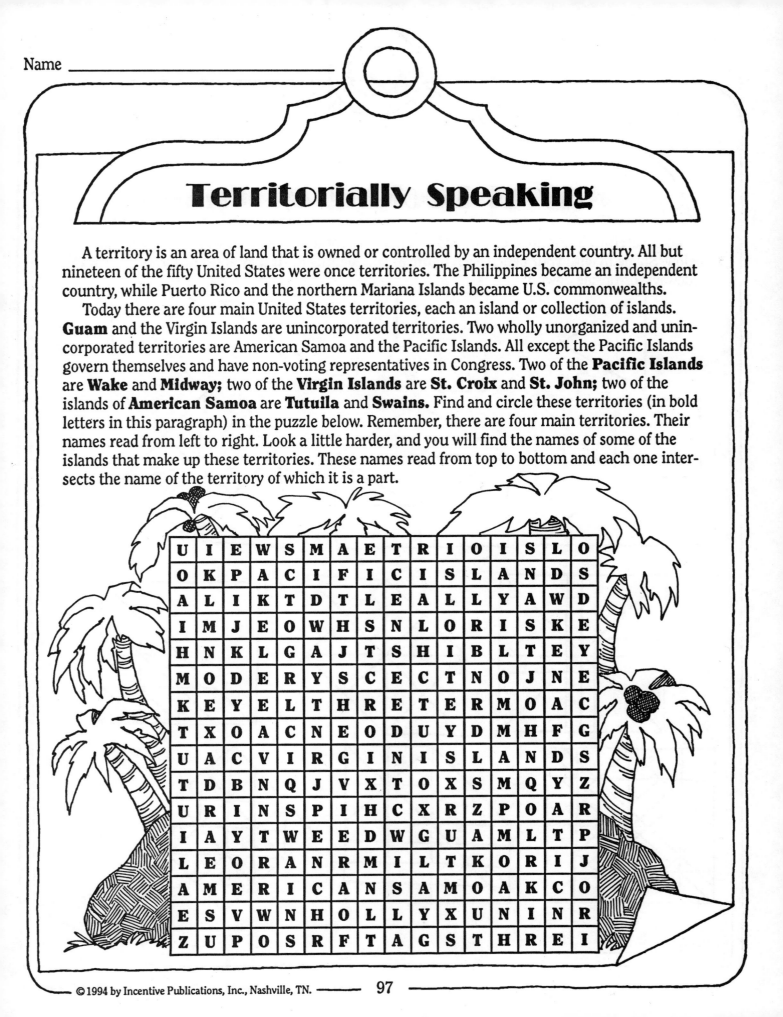

U	I	E	W	S	M	A	E	T	R	I	O	I	S	L	O
O	K	P	A	C	I	F	I	C	I	S	L	A	N	D	S
A	L	I	K	T	D	T	L	E	A	L	L	Y	A	W	D
I	M	J	E	O	W	H	S	N	L	O	R	I	S	K	E
H	N	K	L	G	A	J	T	S	H	I	B	L	T	E	Y
M	O	D	E	R	Y	S	C	E	C	T	N	O	J	N	E
K	E	Y	E	L	T	H	R	E	T	E	R	M	O	A	C
T	X	O	A	C	N	E	O	D	U	Y	D	M	H	F	G
U	A	C	V	I	R	G	I	N	I	S	L	A	N	D	S
T	D	B	N	Q	J	V	X	T	O	X	S	M	Q	Y	Z
U	R	I	N	S	P	I	H	C	X	R	Z	P	O	A	R
I	A	Y	T	W	E	E	D	W	G	U	A	M	L	T	P
L	E	O	R	A	N	R	M	I	L	T	K	O	R	I	J
A	M	E	R	I	C	A	N	S	A	M	O	A	K	C	O
E	S	V	W	N	H	O	L	L	Y	X	U	N	I	N	R
Z	U	P	O	S	R	F	T	A	G	S	T	H	R	E	I

Another
Way of Looking at Things

Look carefully at Figures A, B, C, and D. They are repeated in various ways in the nine boxes below. Shade in with your pencil each figure as you identify it. (It may appear backward, forward, sideways, or upside down.)

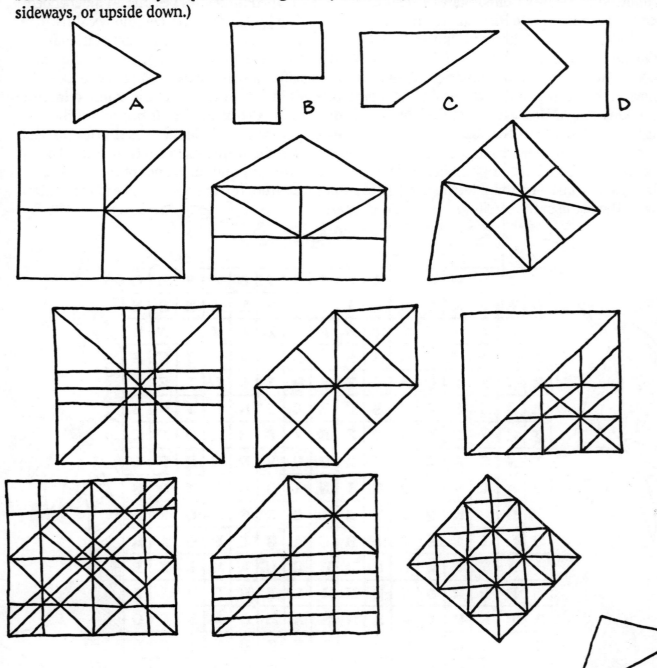

Name _____

FRIENDLY FEELINGS

Ask a friend to play this game with you.

START

Rules:

1. The first player writes a word that names a way good friends should feel about each other. One letter must fit into each square. The player circles the last letter of the word and writes his or her initials there.

2. The second player thinks of a "friendly feeling" word that begins with the circled letter and writes it in the following squares, circling the last letter and placing his or her initials there. The game continues until all the squares are filled or neither player can think of another word.

3. Each filled square counts one point. The player with the highest score wins the game. (Players will want to write long words as they are worth more points.)

4. To get started, you might want to use one of these: trusting, thoughtful, kind.

5. Just for fun, turn the game around and play it with "unfriendly feeling" words.

Name _____

From *The Me I'm Learning to Be* by Imogene Forte. Nashville, TN: Incentive Publications, 1991.

Twenty-Five Systems for Encoding or Ciphering

1. Relate each letter of the message to the letter which follows it in the alphabet.

HELP = IFMQ

2. Relate each letter of the message to the letter preceding it in the alphabet.

HELP = GDKO

3. Relate each letter of the message to a letter of the alphabet which is a certain interval away from the original letter (i.e., five letters following or three letters preceding it in the alphabet).

HELP = MJQU or EBIM

4. Relate each letter to the letter of the alphabet which is the same distance from the end of the alphabet as this letter is from the beginning (i.e., A = Z; B = Y; C = X, etc.).

HELP = SVOK

5. Relate each letter to the numeral that denotes its sequence in the alphabet (i.e., A = 1, B = 2, etc.).

HELP = 8, 5, 12, 16

6. Relate each letter to a double letter code consisting of the letter preceding it and the letter following it in the alphabet (i.e., A = ZB, B = AC, etc.).

HELP = GI, DF, KM, OQ

7. Relate each letter of the alphabet to a code word. (The code word may or may not begin with that letter.)

HELP = HORSES EAT LITTLE PEOPLE.

8. Relate each letter of the alphabet to a special pictorial system

(i.e., **H** = 𝄞𝄞 ; **E** = ϡ ; **L** = 𝅘 ; **P** = 🖐).

HELP = 𝄞𝄞 ϡ 𝅘 🖐

9. Use the multiplication tables to construct a matrix; assign a letter or word to each product of the matrix. Then use the multipliers as your code.

HELP = 4x1, 3x4, 4x4, 1x7.

10. Use a simple grid like this one:

Assign a letter or word to each section. Note that each section has a different border. Use these borders as your code.

H	O	T
B	E	P
S	A	L

HELP = ⌐□⌐⌐

11. Relate each letter to a color. Use colored squares or dots to write your message.
(**H** = ▨ ; **E** = ▦ ; **L** = □ ; **P** = ◪).
HELP = ▨▦□◪

12. Relate each letter to a part of your body. To send a message, merely point to the proper parts in sequence.

13. Relate each letter to a body movement. Then, dance your message!

14. Relate each letter to a three-dimensional item. (Each item might end with the letter it represents.) Keep these items in a code kit or box. When you are ready to send a message, spell it out with these items.

HELP = 🪣🎀👟🍬

15. Create a flag to correlate with each letter of the alphabet. Then use the flags to send your message.

16. Use the dot-dash International Morse Code system, and write your message.
HELP = ...-.. .-.

17. Use the Morse Code with a flashlight or spotlight.

18. Use the Braille System as your base code. Use cardboard or heavy paper and a large pin for writing your message.

HELP = ⠓ ⠑ ⠇ ⠏

19. Create a system of sounds, one to represent each letter, or one to represent each sound in the language. Send your message in a series of sounds.

20. To send a message that self-destructs, create a taste code! Use flavors and textures of food. (You might use a different flavor of lollipop for each vowel, and a different flavor of cracker, cookie, or chip for each consonant.) Then the receiver may eat the message!

21. In the same manner as #20, create a texture or shape code which can be read blind-folded by tactile means.

22. Assign the name of an animal to each letter of the alphabet (i.e., A = Ant, B = Bat, C = Cat, etc.). Use either the name or a picture of each animal to write your message.
HELP = HORSE ELEPHANT LION PUMA

23. Arrange the letters of your message in 5- or 6-letter groups. Then reverse the order of the letters in each group.

>**Message: Leave keys in the box.**
>**Step #1: leavek eysi ntheb ox.**
>**Step #2: kevael isye behtn xo.**

24. Write your message so that every fifth letter should be extracted to spell out the encoded message.

>**HELP = trutH is thE only Law suPreme.**

25. Graph your message. Predetermine a position on the graph for each letter. Then write your message by tracing the points on the graph.

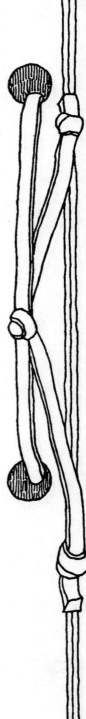

A				
B				
C				
D				
E				
F				
G				
H				
I				
J				
K				
L				
M				
N				
O				
P				
Q				
R				
S				
T				
U				
V				
W				
X				
Y				
Z				

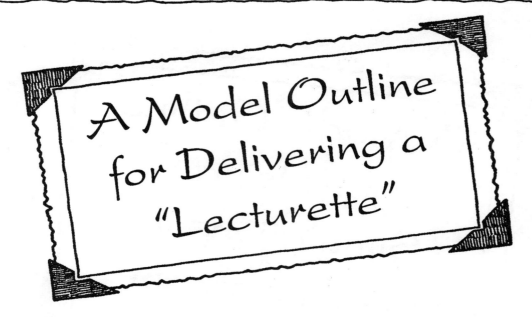

A Model Outline for Delivering a "Lecturette"

OVERVIEW OF "LECTURETTES"

There are six different types of "lecturettes" which are effective with middle level students. These are . . .

1. **The Feedback Lecture:** Give a "lecturette" of ten minutes. Divide students into "lecture study groups" and have them complete a predetermined task based on information given during the "lecturette."

2. **The Guided Lecture:** Give a "lecturette" of ten minutes after providing students with a list of its objectives ahead of time. They are not to take notes until the end of the "lecturette" when they write down everything they can remember for five minutes. Next, students work with a partner to fill in any "information gaps."

3. **The Responsive Lecture:** Students generate questions of their own which form the content of a "lecturette" lasting from ten to twenty minutes.

4. **The Demonstration Lecture:** Give a "lecturette" of approximately twenty minutes that focuses on an interactive demonstration of information to be presented.

5. **The Pause Procedure Lecture:** Give a "lecturette" of twenty minutes, pausing after the first ten minutes of information. Give the students two minutes to share their notes with a peer to fill in any gaps at this time.

6. **The Think/Write/Discuss Lecture:** Give students three questions during a "lecturette" of twenty minutes—one question before, during, and after the "lecturette" itself. Have students write down a response to each question and share results with a peer. Collect papers at end of "lecturette" for personal comments on feedback.

STEPS FOR PREPARING A "LECTURETTE"

1. Decide on topic and objectives for the "lecturette."

2. Decide on length and type of "lecturette."

3. Prepare an outline or set of notes for "lecturette." You may want to make these available to students before or after your delivery for reference or use as a study aid.

4. Write out all introductory and follow-up questions for "lecturette" using Bloom's Taxonomy (or some other higher order thinking skill structure).

5. Allow time for student-generated questions and answers throughout the "lecturette."

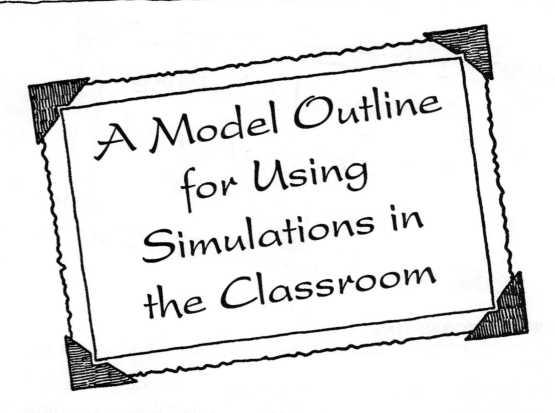

A Model Outline for Using Simulations in the Classroom

OVERVIEW OF SIMULATIONS

A simulation is a model of a physical or social situation in which players assume roles, interact with other players, and make decisions based on those roles and interactions. The simulated model, once constructed, is placed within the context of a game that involves players in a contest, operating under specific rules, to gain an objective. There are several advantages to simulations. (1) Students enjoy simulations with their gaming aspects which become a motivation for learning. (2) Simulating removes the judging aspect from the teacher's role because outcomes are determined by the game itself. (3) Simulations give students the option of gaining true-to-life experiences where they can learn the consequences of actions and situations without actually suffering them. (4) Simulations provide students with an "active" and not a "passive" opportunity for learning basic skills and concepts. Disadvantages of simulation activities include cost of commercial products, time for implementation and debriefing of simulation objectives, lack of guidelines for simulation development, and threat to teachers who want to be "sage on the stage" instead of "guide on the side."

STEPS FOR SELECTING/ADAPTING/DEVELOPING A SIMULATION

1. Consider the cost of the simulation in terms of dollars and time for development and/or implementation.

2. Determine which areas of the curriculum best lend themselves to a simulation and choose a problem situation that is most appropriate for your content objectives.

3. Decide on the numbers, roles, and responsibilities of students who will engage in the simulation activity.

4. Review and/or establish rules and guidelines for the simulation so that adequate decision-making, problem-solving, and communication skills are required of the student participants.

5. Provide adequate time for briefing and debriefing of students about the simulation's required materials, space needs, time allocations, role allocations, and assessment criteria.

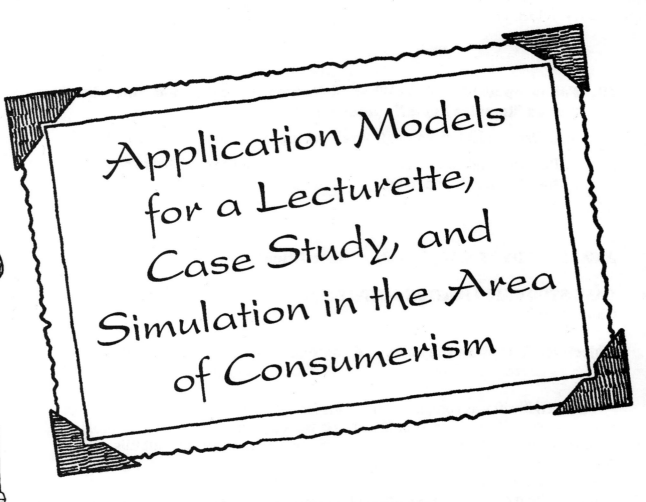

Application Models for a Lecturette, Case Study, and Simulation in the Area of Consumerism

OUTLINE FOR WRITE/THINK/DISCUSS LECTURETTE

Consumer Spending and Buying Habits of Teenagers

I. **Introductory Writing Task: How have you been a consumer of goods and/or services during the past 24 hours? (Application Level)**

    A. Review definitions: consumer, producer, goods, and services.

    B. Share student responses from Introductory Writing Task and classify as goods or services.

    C. Introduce concept of "value" and relate to student purchases during past 24 hours.

    D. Summarize data on teenage spending habits from the National Center for Economic Education over the past three years and note emerging consumer trends.

II. **Reactionary Writing Task: What are three things you need to keep in mind when shopping for a good value? (Comprehension Level)**

    A. Share student responses to Reactionary Writing Task.

    B. Establish criteria for spending money wisely.

    C. Introduce concept of "impulse buying" and compare with criteria for spending money wisely.

III. Follow-up Writing Task: What advice would you give someone who was an "impulse buyer?" (Analysis Level)

A. Collect student responses from all writing tasks and review information.

B. Prepare tomorrow's lecturette on consumer problems related to teenage spending habits and trends.

A CASE STUDY "The High Costs of Shoplifting"

CASE STUDY APPLICATION ACTIVITY: "The Consumer Costs of Shoplifting"

Objective: To explore the costs and complications of "shoplifting" in the retail market.

Mr. Spendthrift was completing his plans for opening a new teenage boutique in a resort area on the west coast of Florida. He was very concerned about the problem of shoplifting since it was becoming a common occurrence throughout this retail community. One of his business partners suggested that he consider using hidden television cameras or security personnel disguised as young customers in the store to reduce the monetary losses from shoplifting. His teenage daughter felt that the use of sensor detectors was still the best deterrent today since it was used in most of the local department stores. Mr. Spendthrift was also debating the types of merchandise to carry in his store which, of course, would influence his choice of security measures. The question was whether he wanted to limit the boutique merchandise to clothing and fashion accessories or whether he wanted to have more variety and also sell things like souvenirs and leisure time products that were popular with today's teenagers. The name of his new boutique would have to reflect the merchandise sold.

DISCUSSION QUESTIONS TO TALK AND WRITE ABOUT

1. What type of merchandise do you think Mr. Spendthrift should sell in his boutique? What information would help you make this decision?

2. If you were Mr. Spendthrift, how would you handle the threat of shoplifters in the boutique?

3. Who pays the "price for shoplifting"? How do you know?

4. If you were the business partner of Mr. Spendthrift, what advice would you give him in naming the boutique and marketing its merchandise to teenagers?

APPLICATION ACTIVITY FOR SIMULATION: Working On An Assembly Line

Objective: To determine the advantages of specialization in producing a product.

DIRECTIONS:
You will be working in cooperative learning groups with five members. Each member of your group will be an employee of a company that makes "Bookmark Bugs." You are to follow the steps below for making your "Bookmark Bug." Each member of your group is to see how many creepy crawlers he or she can make individually within a ten-minute period of time. Wait for the teacher to instruct you on when to begin and when to stop this activity.

Next, your group will organize themselves into an assembly line where each person specializes in performing one step in making the creepy crawlers. When the teacher says "begin," mass produce as many creepy crawlers as you can together in a ten-minute period of time. The way you organize your group and allocate jobs is entirely up to you.

When you have completed both production tasks above, appoint a Recorder and write out your consensus responses to the following questions:

1. Did your group produce more "Bookmark Bugs" as individuals or as a group? Why do you think this was so?

2. Was the quality of your "Bookmark Bugs" any better when produced by individuals or by the group? How do you account for this?

3. What do you think are the advantages and disadvantages of specialization in the production of a given consumer good?

4. What rules or guidelines would you suggest a work team follow in mass-producing a product?

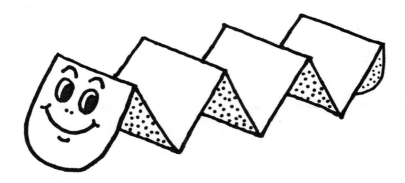

DIRECTIONS FOR ASSEMBLY LINE ACTIVITY
"MASS-PRODUCING A BUG THAT WON'T BITE"

To make this unusual critter, you will need the following materials:
- Construction paper   • Crayons   • Scissors   • Ruler   • Pencil

When you have gathered these materials, you are to do the following:

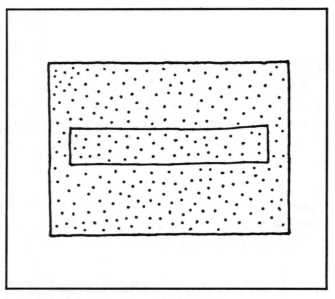

1. Use the ruler to draw a long rectangle that is eight inches long and one inch wide.

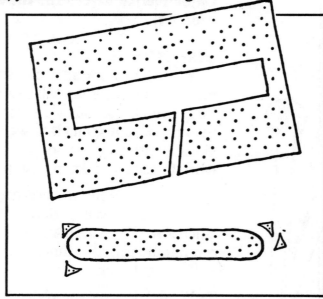

2. With the scissors, cut out the rectangle and round off the ends.

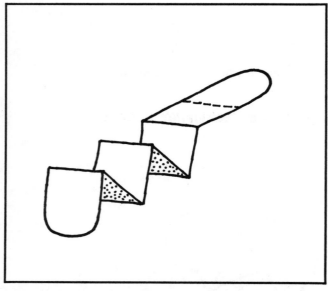

3. Bend the rectangle back and forth about one inch apart so that you have 7- to 8-inch folds from one end to the other.

4. With the black crayon, draw a simple face on the "bug that won't bite."

5. Use the other crayons in your box or collection to decorate your bug with a specific pattern that will help camouflage it from its predators. Be sure your body design can be replicated over and over again.

Planning Worksheet for an Impromptu Speech

"Don't Put Your Foot in Your Mouth"

RECORDING SHEET: "Don't Put Your Foot In Your Mouth"
Objective: To plan and practice speaking skills through impromptu speeches.

Name of Recorder: _____

Names of Group Members: _____

DIRECTIONS:

1. Define "impromptu speech." _____
_____
_____

2. What things would you look for in a good impromptu speech? List them.
_____
_____
_____

3. List ten topics that would be appropriate for impromptu speeches in your classroom.
_____
_____
_____

4. Select a topic from the list on which to give a short two-minute impromptu speech. Be sure to follow this outline in your speech:
   a. Introduce topic in an "attention-grabbing" manner.
   b. State a main idea with supporting details about your topic. Try to include both facts and opinions.
   c. State another main idea with supporting details about your topic if time permits.
   d. Give a strong summarizing idea or "punch line" on the topic.

5. Use your list from question two to evaluate your plan.

6. Present your speech.

Name _____

Tangram Geometry
A Cooperative Learning Activity

PURPOSE:
To use a set of tangrams for exploring basic geometric shapes and figures.

MATERIALS NEEDED:
Set of tangrams and storage envelope for each student
Pair of scissors for group
Set of tangram task cards for group
Paper and pencil

SUGGESTED GROUP SIZE:
Three

SUGGESTED GROUP ROLES:
Coordinator, Timekeeper, and Recorder

SUGGESTED SOCIAL SKILLS:
Sharing information and skills

DIRECTIONS FOR STUDENTS:
1. Use the pattern on Task Card One to make a set of tangrams for each group member according to directions given.
2. Work with your group to complete each of the four remaining Task Cards in the order given.
3. Place all the written work from each group member in the group folder. Be sure each piece of written work has the appropriate group member's name on it.

BONUS GROUP PROJECT OPTION:
As a group, complete Task Card Six, making certain to include the best thinking and writing of all group members.

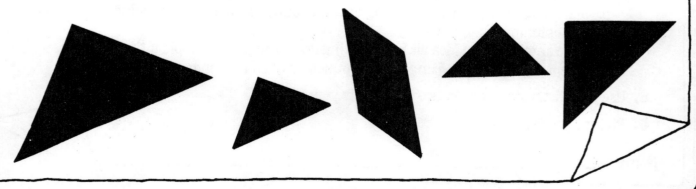

TASK CARD #2

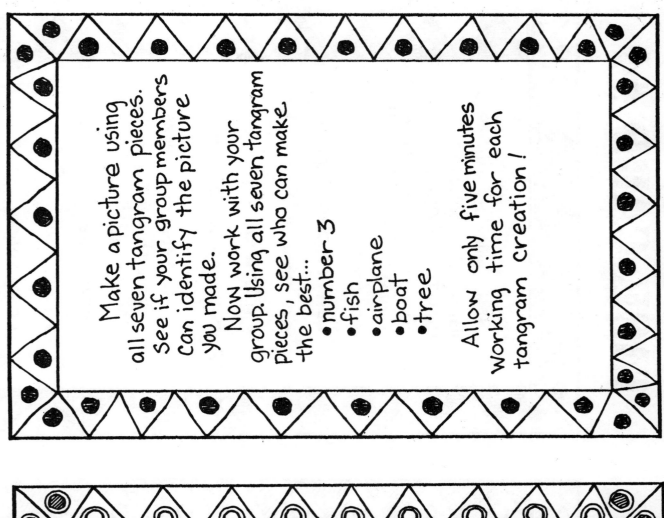

Make a picture using all seven tangram pieces. See if your group members can identify the picture you made.

Now work with your group. Using all seven tangram pieces, see who can make the best...
- number 3
- fish
- airplane
- boat
- tree

Allow only five minutes working time for each tangram creation!

TASK CARD #1

You will need to use a set of tangram pieces to complete the activities in this pocket packet. To make a set, carefully trace the puzzle shape below onto a heavy piece of paper or tagboard. Cut apart.

Now challenge yourself by trying to put each of the shapes together to form the tangram's original shape.

TASK CARD #4

How clever are you? Make each of the following geometric shapes...

(you can only use 5 tangram pieces for each shape!)

- a parallelogram
- an isosceles trapezoid
- a square
- a triangle

If that was too difficult try this first....

(use only 4 tangram pieces for each shape!)

- a rectangle
- a triangle
- a pentagon
- a hexagon

TASK CARD #3

Practice using all seven of your tangram pieces to create each letter of the alphabet. When you have finished trace the tangram letters which compose your initials. See if each of your group members can fill the initials with tangram pieces.

example:

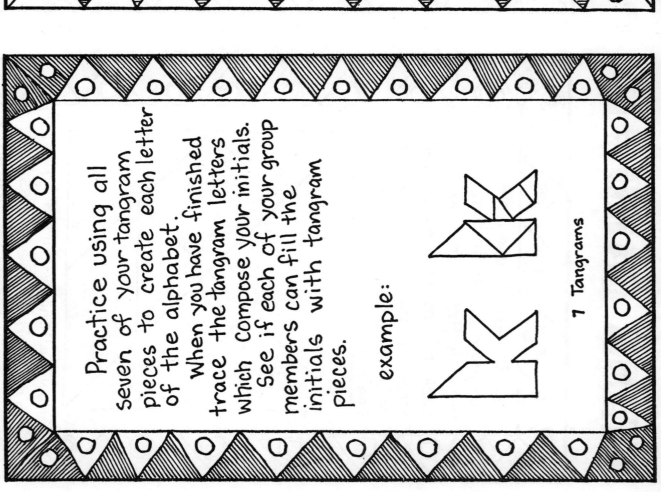

7 Tangrams

TASK CARD #6

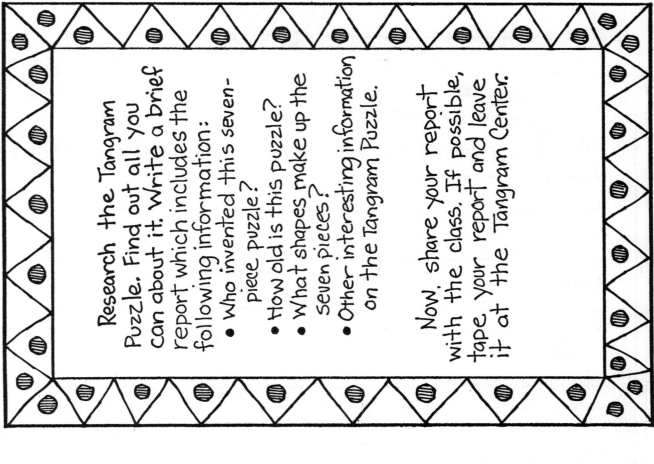

Research the Tangram Puzzle. Find out all you can about it. Write a brief report which includes the following information:

- Who invented this seven-piece puzzle?
- How old is this puzzle?
- What shapes make up the seven pieces?
- Other interesting information on the Tangram Puzzle.

Now, share your report with the class. If possible, tape your report and leave it at the Tangram Center.

TASK CARD #5

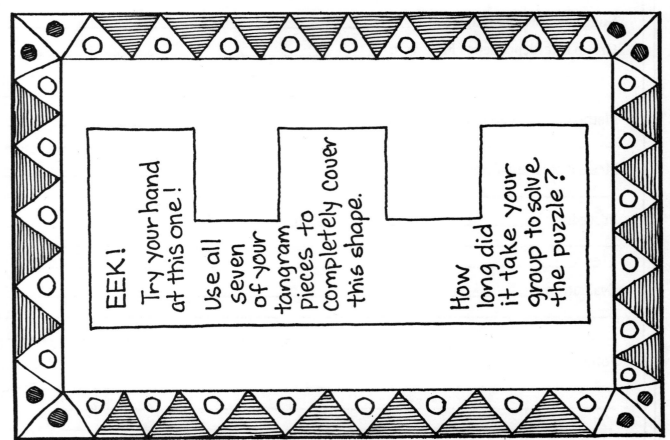

EEK!
Try your hand at this one!

Use all seven of your tangram pieces to completely cover this shape.

How long did it take your group to solve the puzzle?

A Cooperative Learning Lesson Plan

Subject: _____

Purpose: _____
_____

Materials Needed: _____
_____
_____

Suggested Group Size: _____

Suggested Group Roles: _____
_____

Suggested Social Skills Focus: _____

Suggested Study Skills Focus: _____

Group Interdependence Measures: _____
_____
_____

Method of Individual Accountability: _____
_____

Method of Group Accountability: _____
_____

Procedure: _____
_____
_____

Evaluation: _____
_____
_____

Follow-up and Extension: _____
_____
_____
_____

ENCOURAGING THE DEVELOPMENT OF THINKING SKILLS ACROSS THE CURRICULUM

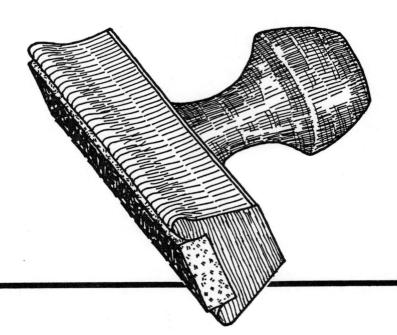

An Introduction to Bloom's Taxonomy of Cognitive Thinking Skills For Students

Bloom's Taxonomy of Cognitive Development is a model that can help you learn how to think critically and systematically. (**Taxonomy** is another word for **structure** or **schemata.**) This taxonomy provides a way to organize thinking skills into six levels. The first level is the most basic or simplest level of thinking and the last level is the most challenging or complex level of thinking.

Each of the six levels of Bloom's Taxonomy can be best understood through the use of several different types of action verbs or behaviors. A list of the thinking levels with corresponding sampler sets of verbs is provided below. After studying this presentation of Bloom's Taxonomy, write an outline of things to do for an independent study topic of interest to you. Choose one verb or behavior from each level of the taxonomy and write a task or activity to complete on the Bloom Lesson Plan Outline which appears on page 119. (Put each activity in a space with its correlating level of thinking.)

BLOOM'S TAXONOMY OF CRITICAL THINKING SKILLS

KNOWLEDGE LEVEL:
When students think at this level, they are asked to memorize, remember, and recall previously-learned material. Some common verbs or behaviors for this level are: **define, list, identify, label, name, recall, record, draw, recite,** and **reproduce.**

COMPREHENSION LEVEL:
When students think at this level, they are asked to demonstrate their ability to understand the meaning of material learned and to express that meaning in their own words. Some common verbs or behaviors for this level are: **explain, describe, summarize, give examples, classify, find, measure, prepare, retell, reword, rewrite,** and **show.**

APPLICATION LEVEL:
When students think at this level, they are asked to use learned material in a situation different from the situation in which the material was taught. Some common verbs or behaviors for this level are: **apply, compute, construct, develop, discuss, generalize, interview, investigate, model, perform, plan, present, produce, prove, solve,** and **use.**

Bloom's Taxonomy, Page 2

ANALYSIS LEVEL:
> When students think at this level, they are asked to break down material (ideas and concepts) into its component parts so that the organization and relationships between parts is better recognized and understood. Some common verbs or behaviors for this level are: **compare and contrast, criticize, debate, determine, diagram, differentiate, discover, draw conclusions, examine, infer, search, survey,** and **sort.**

SYNTHESIS LEVEL:
> When students think at this level, they are asked to put together parts of the material to form a new and different whole. Synthesis is the exact opposite of analysis. Some common verbs or behaviors for this level are: **build, combine, create, design, imagine, invent, make up, produce, propose,** and **present.**

EVALUATION LEVEL:
> When students think at this level, they are asked to judge the value of material (a statement, novel, poem, research finding, fact) for a given purpose. All judgments are to be based on a set of clearly defined criteria whose outcomes can be defended or validated. Some common verbs or behaviors for this level are: **assess, critique, defend, evaluate, grade, judge, measure, rank, recommend, select, test, validate,** and **verify.**

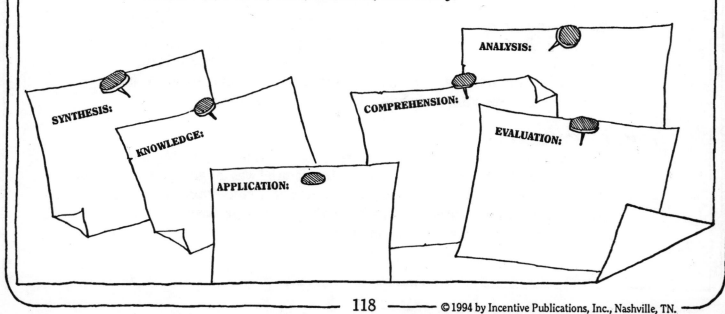

BLOOM'S
LESSON PLAN OUTLINE

Title _____

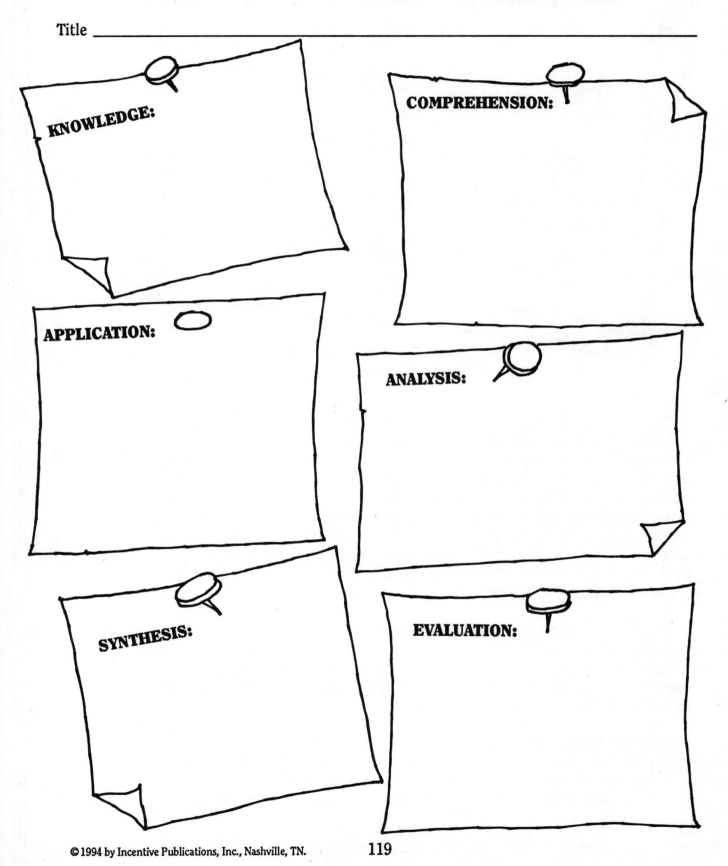

KNOWLEDGE:

COMPREHENSION:

APPLICATION:

ANALYSIS:

SYNTHESIS:

EVALUATION:

Using Bloom's Taxonomy of Thinking Skills To Make the Most of the Media Center

The school media center provides a treasure trove of often-taken-for-granted and underutilized teaching resources that offer endless opportunities for creative lessons and mind-stretching projects. By re-examining some of these materials, creative media center directors and teachers may enable students to complete exciting learning challenges, add to their storehouse of knowledge, and improve research skills and abilities. As students begin to use media center materials as the pivotal point for cooperative learning projects, science-, social studies-, and literature-based mind-stretchers, and independent research projects in keeping with their own special interests, the media center will quickly become more than just the place you go to "look it up."

On the following pages, you will find one-dozen mind-stretching research projects, each based on Bloom's Taxonomy and featuring a media center research project. These worksheets have been designed to promote positive and productive use of the media center materials and to encourage creative and critical thinking, research, and inquiry skills.

After completing some or all of the media center mind-stretchers presented on pages 121–132, more ambitious students will be ready to create and use mind-stretchers in keeping with their unique needs and interests. The reproducible lesson plan outline on page 119 is designed for both teacher and student use.

The Amazing Almanac

KNOWLEDGE:
Record an interesting piece of information from the almanac that begins with each letter of the word ALMANAC.

A _____

L _____

M _____

A _____

N _____

A _____

C _____

COMPREHENSION:
In your own words, summarize how the almanac can be of interest or use to students like yourself.

APPLICATION:
Interview ten people to find out if and when they use the almanac. Record your findings in chart or graph form.

ANALYSIS:
Survey the Farmer's Almanac and determine how it is like and how it is different from the almanac in your school library.

SYNTHESIS:
Develop an almanac with a special theme for your class. Consider a Community Almanac, a School Almanac, or a Teenage Almanac.

EVALUATION:
Imagine you can take only one reference book from the media center on a space flight. Justify or criticize the choice of an almanac for this purpose.

Card Catalog Countdown

KNOWLEDGE:
Answer the following question.
What is the purpose of the card catalog in the school's media center?

COMPREHENSION:
Draw a flow chart to show how one finds a particular book in the card catalog.

APPLICATION:
Construct a quiz to test one's ability to understand and use the card catalog effectively.

ANALYSIS:
Survey at least ten students in your class to find out how and when they use the card catalog in their work. From your survey results, try to determine the characteristics that make it likely that a student will make good use of this tool. Then determine the characteristics that make it likely a student will overlook the use of this tool in the learning process.

SYNTHESIS:
Make up an unusual design or blueprint for a new card catalog section of the media center. Try to make it creative so that it will have appeal for the student who will use it.

EVALUATION:
Criticize the ways the use of the card catalog is taught as a skill in your school. Recommend ways to improve the teaching/learning process for this concept.

SYNTHESIS:

KNOWLEDGE:

APPLICATION:

COMPREHENSION:

ANALYSIS:

EVALUATION:

Dictionary Dialogue

KNOWLEDGE:
Record at least ten types of information that one can find in a dictionary.

COMPREHENSION:
Choose a word and draw a simple mini-poster to show the standard format and information one can expect to find in a typical dictionary entry.

APPLICATION:
Construct a simple quiz to determine what classmates do and do not understand about use of the dictionary. Include a bonus question or two.

ANALYSIS:
Select words from the dictionary that reflect a particular ethnic culture such as French, Latin, or Spanish. Discover which types of words from other languages are most likely to become part of the English language. Write down your conclusions and give examples to support your findings.

SYNTHESIS:
Create a dictionary of slang that is popular with teenagers today. Follow the traditional format for dictionary entries.

EVALUATION:
Rank order the dictionary, the atlas, and the encyclopedia according to their importance to students. What criteria will you use and what reasons can you give for your choice?

SYNTHESIS:

KNOWLEDGE:

APPLICATION:

COMPREHENSION:

ANALYSIS:

EVALUATION:

Directory Decisions

KNOWLEDGE:

List all of the places one might reasonably expect to find a directory in his or her community.

COMPREHENSION:

Briefly explain how a directory can save time when you find yourself in each of the following places.

a. Office building _____

_____

b. Museum _____

_____

c. Apartment complex _____

_____

d. Department store _____

_____

e. Library _____

_____

APPLICATION:

Construct a directory for your school.

ANALYSIS:

Bring in a directory and examine its purpose, format, and copy. Write down three of its strengths and three ways it could be improved.

SYNTHESIS:

Imagine a world without a telephone directory. Predict all of the problems that would result from such a situation. Next, list an alternative way in which to obtain a person's telephone number.

EVALUATION:

Establish a set of criteria for a good directory. Ask each student to bring in a directory from home and rate each directory according to the established criteria.

Encyclopedia Encore

KNOWLEDGE:
Identify three different encyclopedia publishers and write down information about each one.

COMPREHENSION:
Summarize the problems students have when abusing or overusing the encyclopedia while doing a classroom assignment.

APPLICATION:
Produce an Encyclopedia Treasure Hunt for classmates to use in practicing their research skills.

ANALYSIS:
Compare and contrast the three encyclopedias listed in the Knowledge Activity.

SYNTHESIS:
Make up a magazine ad for one of the three encyclopedias of the Knowledge Activity that has special appeal to teenagers.

EVALUATION:
Decide when an encyclopedia is the best reference tool to use and when it is the least effective reference tool to use when completing a homework assignment.

Graphs Galore

KNOWLEDGE:

Use magazines and newspapers to find a wide assortment of graphs. State the main purpose of or types of information given in each graph.

COMPREHENSION:

Classify your collection of graphs in at least three different ways. Explain the rationale for your grouping.

APPLICATION:

Construct a pie graph to show how you would like to spend a perfect twenty-four-hour day.

ANALYSIS:

How is a graph like a road map? like a blueprint? like a photograph?

SYNTHESIS:

Write a story that has one of the following titles:
The Missing Graph
The Graph that Changed the World
A Piece of the Pie

EVALUATION:

Defend the following statement.
A graph is the BEST way to present information to a reader.

Maps, Globes, and Atlases

KNOWLEDGE:
Identify all the different types of information you can find on a map. Try coming up with an idea for each letter of the alphabet. Example: D is for distances between cities.

COMPREHENSION:
Randomly select twenty different places on a United States map. Write your choices down and group or categorize them in some way. Describe your classification scheme. Ask a friend to do the same, then exchange your lists. Are your groupings alike or different?

APPLICATION:
Plan a five-day trip in your state. Where will you go and what will you do? How will you get there and how will you move about? What will it cost and how will you budget your dollars?

ANALYSIS:
Compare and contrast a world map, a globe, and an atlas. List the advantages and disadvantages of each. Tell when one might be a more effective tool to use than another.

SYNTHESIS:
Invent a new country. Describe its size, population, location, and topography. Tell about its people, its lifestyle, its government, and its economy.

EVALUATION:
In your opinion, what should be the eighth wonder of the world? What criteria will you use and what defense can you give to validate your choice?

SYNTHESIS:

KNOWLEDGE:

APPLICATION:

ANALYSIS:

COMPREHENSION:

EVALUATION:

Microfiche Memo

KNOWLEDGE:

What is a microfiche and why should one know how to use it effectively?

COMPREHENSION:

Outline a report for a class using microfiche as your primary reference source.

APPLICATION:

Show someone how to use microfiche in the library by producing a comic strip, filmstrip, mural, picture book, flowchart, or personal demonstration.

ANALYSIS:

Compare and contrast microfiche with the card catalog. Determine when and under what circumstances one is more efficient than the other.

SYNTHESIS:

Compose a flyer, advertisement, poster, or announcement to promote more widespread use of microfiche among students.

EVALUATION:

Grade the microfiche collection in your school or public library. What rating scale and criteria will you use?

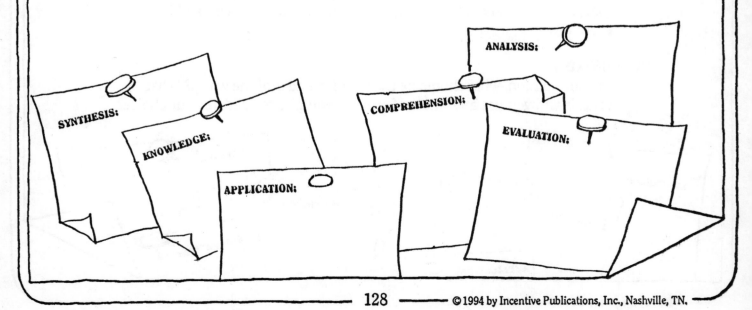

Periodic Table Talk

KNOWLEDGE:
List the elements of the periodic table.

COMPREHENSION:
Explain how the periodic table can be of great use to scientists, environmentalists, or archeologists.

APPLICATION:
Demonstrate how you might use the periodic table in a science project, a science fair, or a science lab.

ANALYSIS:
Compare and contrast any two elements of the periodic table. Do this in graph or chart form.

SYNTHESIS:
Devise a simple lesson plan to teach a friend something about the periodic table. Your lesson plan should have the following parts:
- Objective
- Time
- Materials Needed
- Procedure
- Follow-up

Use it to "educate" your friend.

EVALUATION:
Judge the quality of your lesson plan by answering the following questions.
1. Were my objectives relevant and realistic in terms of intent and number?
2. Was I enthusiastic in my delivery?
3. Was I well prepared and well organized?
4. Did my friend understand what he or she was doing and why he or she was doing it?
5. Were my directions clear and to the point?
6. Did I enjoy working with my friend during this lesson?
7. Would I do anything differently next time when presenting this lesson?

Reading The Reader's Guide

KNOWLEDGE:
Find the *Reader's Guide to Periodical Literature* in the library and write down the name of its editor, publisher, and copyright date.

COMPREHENSION:
Summarize how you might use the *Reader's Guide* to save time when doing a report.

APPLICATION:
Use the *Reader's Guide* to locate three different articles from three different publications on a single topic of your choice. Write a one-paragraph summary for each article.

ANALYSIS:
Survey the *Reader's Guide* and decide on five magazines or newspapers that you would most like to have access to in your school library. Write down their names and give a reason for each one.

SYNTHESIS:
Make up a tee-shirt designed to celebrate National Reading Week.

EVALUATION:
Decide which of the following criteria would be most important to you when selecting three articles for a research report.

- Length of article
- Author of article
- Title of article
- Source of article
- Information presented in article
- Readability of article
- Use of visual aids in article (photographs, tables, charts, diagrams, etc.)

Thesaurus Talk-Back

KNOWLEDGE:

Write down three synonyms for each of the following overused words in kids' writing.

said _____ _____ _____

like _____ _____ _____

walked _____ _____ _____

ran _____ _____ _____

COMPREHENSION:

Use one of the synonyms written down for each word in the Knowledge Activity to write a set of complete sentences.

APPLICATION:

Use a thesaurus to rewrite each of these proverbs so they are hardly recognizable.

Too many cooks spoil the broth. _____

_____

A rolling stone gathers no moss. _____

_____

Don't cut off your nose to spite your face. _____

_____

ANALYSIS:

Examine pages from your favorite book and select several common words. Use the thesaurus to substitute synonyms for these words and decide if the meaning is changed in any way.

SYNTHESIS:

Create an ad for a talking or electronic thesaurus of the future. Tell the wonderful things it can do for students.

EVALUATION:

Write a persuasive paragraph convincing parents that a thesaurus is important for their children to have.

The Media Center Wrap-up

KNOWLEDGE:
Record all of the different types of reference tools that are available to you in your school library/media center.

COMPREHENSION:
In your own words, tell why it is more important today for students to have good library skills than it was for their ancestors. Give as many reasons as you can.

APPLICATION:
Interview the librarian or media specialist in your school to find out more about him or her. Write a set of questions to use during the interview. Later, write the interviewee's responses in paragraph form.

ANALYSIS:
Discover why libraries are now called media centers in most schools.

SYNTHESIS:
Create a skit to show appropriate and inappropriate uses of, and behavior in, the school library/media center.

EVALUATION:
Judge the quality of your school library/media center. What criteria will you use? What measures will you employ? What recommendations for improvement will you make?

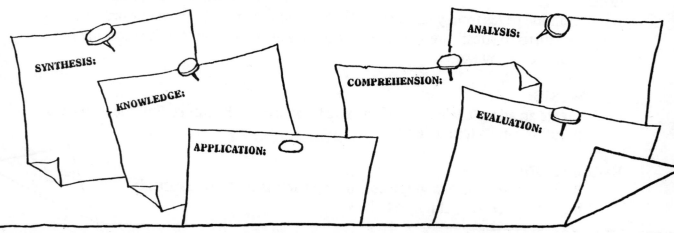

An Introduction to Williams' Taxonomy of Divergent Thinking and Feeling for Students

Did you know that there are eight different things you can do when you put on your "creative thinking hat?" This hierarchy of thinking skill levels is outlined for you below. Read about each skill level and do the "practice" activity suggested for each one.

Fluency Level:

When you practice creative thinking at this level, you try to come up with lots of ideas, oodles of responses, scads of choices, or many ways to do something.

In two minutes, make a list of all the different "red" things you can think of.

Flexibility Level:

When you practice creative thinking at this level, you try to find many different and varied categories of ideas and situations.

In two minutes, classify your list of "red" things in some way. How many different categories of ideas and situations do you have? Can you add others to make it a more comprehensive list of "red" things?

Originality Level:

When you practice creative thinking at this level, you try to come up with the most unusual and original idea that you can think of.

In two minutes, try to come up with some "red" things that nobody else in your group or class has thought of. Try to come up with clever ideas.

Elaboration Level:

When you practice creative thinking at this level, you try to stretch your mind and tease your imagination by expanding, enlarging, or adding details to elaborate on your best idea(s).

In two minutes, add details to your most original and novel "red" thing from the previous activity. Tell what it looks like, smells like, tastes like, feels like, and sounds like.

Risk Taking Level:

When you practice creative thinking at this level, you try new challenges and explore new situations that often involve taking some personal chances or risks.

In two minutes, tell about a time when you were so angry at someone or something that you saw "red."

Complexity Level:

When you practice creative thinking at this level, you try to make sense of some complicated idea or bring structure to a complex situation.

In two minutes, try to explain why the color "red" is often selected to represent conflicting emotions such as love and anger.

Curiosity Level:

When you practice creative thinking at this level, you try to follow a hunch, ponder a point, or wonder about alternatives in a given situation or experience.

In two minutes, think of a series of questions you might want to have answered about the circulatory system of your body and the "red" blood that makes it all function properly.

Imagination Level:

When you practice creative thinking at this level, you try to visualize, dream, and wonder about things that do not exist or that are mere fantasies at this point.

In two minutes, imagine what would happen if everything in the world were "red" in color.

Adapted from *Creativity Assessment Packet* by Frank Williams. Austin, TX: Pro-Ed Publishers, 1980. Used by permission.

A Lesson Plan
Using Williams' Taxonomy
in a Study of Gender

Directions: Work individually or with a small group to complete the following creative thinking activities dealing with "gender" issues in today's society.

FLUENCY:

Make a list of important or famous American women who have made their places in history.

FLEXIBILITY:

Think of all the American women who are not considered famous or important but who have, in your opinion, contributed to significant historical events and changes in your home, school, community, or country.

ORIGINALITY:

What do you think is the most unusual, or "unobvious," contribution that women have made to the American dream or culture? Give reasons for your choice.

ELABORATION:

Build on this idea: "Boys are taught to apologize for their weaknesses, girls for their strengths" (adapted from a quotation from Lois Wyse).

RISK TAKING:

What do you enjoy (or would you enjoy) most about being a female in the United States today?

COMPLEXITY:

Assume you have been elected by the student body as official spokesperson for your peers in casting the deciding vote in determining whether or not your school should hire a female principal. If you knew that your deeply felt position on this issue were contrary to that held by the vast majority of the student voters you represent, would you cast your vote according to your beliefs or theirs?

CURIOSITY:

If you could meet the most famous female athlete, entertainer, or political figure of your choice, what things would you want to inquire of her?

IMAGINATION:

Imagine that a woman was just elected President of the United States. How might her leadership style differ from those of her male predecessors?

A Lesson Plan
Using Williams' Taxonomy
in a Study of Cultural Diversity

Directions: Work individually or with a small group to complete the following creative thinking activities dealing with "cultural diversity" issues in today's society.

FLUENCY:
List all of the words you can think of related to the idea of cultural diversity.

FLEXIBILITY:
Categorize your list of words in some way, adding other words for variety and clarity where necessary to complete a vivid and exciting picture of cultural diversity in your classroom and community.

ORIGINALITY:
Invent a new word (or creative combination of existing words) to reflect the meaning of cultural diversity for students.

ELABORATION:
Expand on this idea: "People are isolated in the school or the community because they built walls instead of bridges."

RISK TAKING:
What would you fear most about speaking up in defense of a minority group that you felt was being persecuted in your town or school?

COMPLEXITY:
If you were in charge of deciding who could immigrate to the United States and who could not, would you let in those you thought would make the greatest contributions to our society or those who were most in need of help and refuge?

CURIOSITY:
What questions would you want to ask of someone who had an ethnic background very different from your own?

IMAGINATION:
Visualize a world free of prejudice and cultural bias. What would it look like?

A Lesson Plan
Using Williams' Taxonomy
to Learn More About the Environment

Directions: Work individually or with a small group to complete the following creative thinking activities dealing with environmental issues in today's society.

FLUENCY:
Record lots of reasons young people should become an important part of today's efforts to save the environment.

FLEXIBILITY:
Use your FLUENCY list to write down ways students might assist in the effort to clean up the environment.

ORIGINALITY:
What is the most clever or creative idea you can think of for promoting "student involvement" in local environmental issues and efforts?

ELABORATION:
You see a littered campsite and an empty tent. What do you think happened?

RISK TAKING:
How do you tend to pollute or abuse the environment?

COMPLEXITY:
How and why do you think the United States has become a "throw-away" society?

CURIOSITY:
What do you wonder about when you see such things as polluted beaches, wild animals in captivity at zoos, and trash along the roads and highways?

IMAGINATION:
Imagine your wishes would all come true. What is your ultimate environmental dream or fantasy for the future?

A CALENDAR OF SHORT CREATIVE THINKING TASKS

MONDAY	TUESDAY	WEDNESDAY	THURSDAY	FRIDAY
Stretch your mind and imagine ways that the ocean is like the mountains.	Stretch your imagination and think of all the ways we could improve the design of an umbrella.	Which is more interesting to you, a high skyscraper or a high cliff?	Which do you think is more fascinating, the desert or the rain forest? Explain.	Imagine your eyes are found on your feet; design a pair of glasses for them.
Create an unusual way to classify the friends that you have.	Design a slogan for a pizza parlor that sells only vegetarian pizza.	Create a backpack for a camel.	Think about a situation that puzzles you. Figure out an explanation for it.	If your locker could talk, what would it say?
Make a list of as many words as you can think of to describe a ride on a school bus.	Form as many new words as possible from the letters of the name of your favorite TV hero.	Describe what it would be like if you went to school on weekends and played during the week.	Write a short story about a runaway monkey.	What if it rained cats and dogs?
Create a family of shoes. Assign roles to different types of shoes. Write a play in which the shoes are the actors and actresses in a school situation.	Give five reasons teenagers are special.	Pretend you are a snake that people keep trying to destroy. Write a story about your life.	Create a poem or paragraph by adding lines to this beginning: School is fun, vacation is better.	Devise as many ways as you can to get from one place to another.
Develop a plan of new ways to help spread joy to the world.	Combine the letters B, C, F, T, and Y to make a drawing of a group of insects.	List as many uses for a feather as you can think of.	Expand upon this idea: "Look before you leap."	As a school bully, what would be your greatest fears?

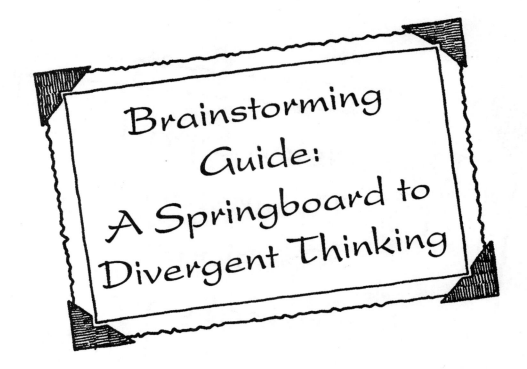

WHY?

The intended result of brainstorming is to generate a large number of ideas which will lead to a larger number of creative solutions to a given problem.

Two secondary benefits are to be derived from this process:

1. Students learn to express their ideas freely, without fear of criticism.
2. Students learn to build upon each other's ideas.

HOW?

There are four requirements for a profitable brainstorming session:

1. All ideas are accepted. Defer judgment and criticism.
2. Participants must feel free to say everything they think and to hold nothing back. The "farther out" the ideas are, the better.
3. Participants build on the ideas of others. (Don't wait for a new idea to come; let it grow out of the last idea given by altering that idea in some way.)
4. Strive for quantity! The more ideas, the better.

FOLLOW-UP

After the brainstorming session:

1. Leave all ideas written as they were recorded.
2. Enlist student participation in setting some standards for evaluating and pruning the collected ideas. (The criteria will depend somewhat on the ultimate goal for use of the ideas.)

   Examples: Is the idea practical?

   Can we really accomplish it?

   Is it compatible with everyday living?

   Does it solve a problem without creating a new one?
3. Discuss which ideas fit the criteria.
4. Decide on ways to develop the ideas (like making a model, diagram, design, drawing, writing descriptive material, etc.).

Discussion Sparkers For Brainstorming Sessions: A Springboard to Divergent Thinking

List as many uses as you can for . . .

Create an ad slogan for . . .

It's hard to believe . . .

What if . . .

Defend . . .

It's best to forget . . .

Describe . . .

Did you know . . .

Design . . .

List ways to conserve . . .

Why do you think . . .

State your position on . . .

That place reminds me of . . .

Tell why . . .

Who knows . . .

Make up a story about . . .

How would you improve . . .

Predict what will happen when . . .

Name people who . . .

Where in the world . . .

List Making: A Springboard to Divergent Thinking

Make a list of ...

1. Nineteen kinds of flying machines
2. A dozen things to do with a kite ... other than fly it on a windy day
3. A dozen root vegetables
4. A dozen fruits with one pit
5. Seven original oxymorons
6. Thirteen words that express joy or happiness
7. Thirty-two uses for a large paper bag
8. The full names of ten well-known sports figures over forty years of age
9. Eighty-eight words that begin with the letter E (don't use the dictionary!)
10. The capitals of sixteen countries other than your own
11. Fifteen good story starters for tall tales and fifteen good story starters for mystery stories
12. Nine famous women and their claims to fame
13. Fifty two-letter words
14. Twenty-five games played with a ball
15. A dozen ways to reuse glass jars
16. Eighteen trees that bear nuts
17. Sixteen gemstones that are used to make jewelry
18. Sixteen ways to make change for one dollar
19. Twenty-two time-saving kitchen devices
20. Twenty-six careers in the health industry
21. Fourteen ways to send information from one country to another
22. Twenty kinds of desserts that contain chocolate
23. Sixteen well-known mountains
24. Twenty-four means of transportation with wheels
25. Thirteen famous inventors or discoverers and their inventions or discoveries
26. Six places where you can locate up-to-date information about the countries of Europe
27. Ten major world seaports
28. A dozen ways to reuse junk mail
29. The names of ten people who have contributed significantly to world peace during the past decade
30. Ten different species of snakes
31. Forty musical instruments
32. Sixteen different languages
33. A dozen TV programs appropriate for pre-teen or teen viewing
34. A dozen ways to express appreciation for someone's thoughtfulness
35. Ten original titles or lists to use as springboards to divergent thinking

An Introduction to the Multiple Intelligences for Students

Did you know there are seven different types of intelligence and that each of us possesses all seven, although one or more of them may be stronger than others? Dr. Howard Gardner, a researcher and professor at the Harvard Graduate School of Education, has developed the Theory of Multiple Intelligences to help us better understand ourselves and the way we acquire information in school. Try to rank order the seven intelligences below as they best describe the way you learn, with "1" being your strongest intelligence area and "7" being your weakest intelligence area. Try to think of examples and instances in the the classroom when you were successful on a test, assignment, activity, or task because it was compatible with the way you like to learn.

_____ **1. LINGUISTIC INTELLIGENCE**

Do you find it easy to memorize information, write poems or stories, give oral talks, read books, play word games like Scrabble and Password, use big words in your conversations or assignments, and remember what you hear?

_____ **2. LOGICAL-MATHEMATICAL INTELLIGENCE**

Do you find it easy to compute numbers in your head and on paper, to solve brainteasers, to do logic puzzles, to conduct science experiments, to figure out number and sequence patterns, and to watch videos or television shows on science and nature themes?

_____ **3. SPATIAL INTELLIGENCE**

Do you find it easy to draw, paint, or doodle, work through puzzles and mazes, build with blocks or various types of building sets, follow maps and flow charts, use a camera to record what you see around you, and prefer reading material that has lots of illustrations?

Name _____

Multiple Intelligences for Students, Page 2

_____ **4. BODILY-KINESTHETIC INTELLIGENCE**

Do you find it easy to engage in lots of sports and physical activities, move around rather than sit still, spend free time outdoors, work with your hands on such things as model-building or sewing, participate in dance, ballet, gymnastics, plays, puppet shows or other performances, and mess around with finger painting, clay, and papier-mâché?

_____ **5. MUSICAL INTELLIGENCE**

Do you find it easy to play a musical instrument or sing in the choir, listen to favorite records or tapes, make up your own songs or raps, recognize off-key recordings or noises, remember television jingles and lyrics of many different songs, and work while listening to or humming simple melodies and tunes?

_____ **6. INTERPERSONAL INTELLIGENCE**

Do you find it easy to make friends, meet strangers, resolve conflicts among peers, lead groups or clubs, engage in gossip, participate in team sports, plan social activities, and teach or counsel others?

_____ **7. INTRAPERSONAL INTELLIGENCE**

Do you find it easy to function independently, do your own work and thinking, spend time alone, engage in solo hobbies and activities, attend personal growth seminars, set goals, analyze your own strengths and weaknesses, and keep private diaries or journals?

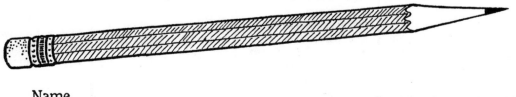

Name _____

ATRIX OF SAMPLE LESSON PLANS FOR TEACHERS USING THE MULTIPLE INTELLIGENCES

	Human Body SCIENCE	Geography SOCIAL STUDIES	Geometry MATHEMATICS	Mythology LANGUAGE ARTS
Verbal/Linguistic	Verbally explain how the eye or the ear functions.	Debate the pros and cons of building nuclear plants in major cities around the world.	Prepare an oral talk about how geometry is reflected in nature.	Write a modern-day version of your favorite myth.
Logical/Mathematical	Predict what would happen if scientists could construct the bionic man or bionic woman.	Follow a recipe to construct a relief map of some important geographical site of interest to you.	Make a chart, diagram, or flow chart to show how one goes about using formulas to determine perimeters and areas of various geometric figures.	Analyze today's advertising messages and determine which names and symbols come from the world of mythology.
Visual/Spatial	Draw a diagram of the heart and label its parts.	Create a series of murals to accurately depict the seven continents.	Create a design for wallpaper, wrapping paper, fabric, or area rug using only geometric shapes and figures.	Draw a series of patterns and images to illustrate several different mythological characters.
Body/Kinesthetic	Act out the scientific processes for each of the body systems.	Teach and play a series of memory games to reinforce major geography concepts such as important bodies of water, capitals of the states, locations of historical landmarks, or facts about the rain forests.	Organize a stand-up spelling bee of geometric words and concepts.	Play "guess what mythological character I am" through a game of charades with your peers.
Musical/Rhythmic	Write a rap song about diseases that affect the young.	Write out a series of facts, stories, and myths about people around the world and select a musical composition to play in the background while you read your information to others.	Decide on a type of music, sound, and rhythm for each geometric shape. Use these to write a simple musical composition.	Work out a simple dance to the story of Pandora who allowed all the evils of the world to escape from a special box, leaving only hope behind.
Interpersonal	Conduct an interview with a doctor, nurse, or dentist.	With a group of students, create a set of haiku poems to reflect the different geographical phenomena of your state, country, or continent.	Invent a new geometric shape and teach others how to use it.	Practice joint storytelling with a friend to tell others about the myths that you have studied.
Intrapersonal	Keep a personal diary of your eating habits for a week.	Imagine having a dialogue with a creature who inhabits the Rain Forest. What would your conversation look like?	Compose a short paragraph telling whether you are more like a circle, a square, a rectangle, or a triangle.	Decide which mythological character you would want to invite to your home for a private dinner and plan the menu as well as the evening's activities.

144

Questions To Find Answers For

1. **Where do butterflies go when it rains?**
   Answer: _____
   _____

2. **When was the Ice Age?**
   Answer: _____
   _____

3. **What is a bathysphere?**
   Answer: _____
   _____

4. **Why are so many lead pencils yellow?**
   Answer: _____
   _____

5. **Where and when was the first attack on the U.S. made during World War II?**
   Answer: _____
   _____

6. **How does a camera work?**
   Answer: _____
   _____

7. **When and where did the first group of people discover that the Earth is round?**
   Answer: _____
   _____

8. **When and where was the United Nations founded?**
   Answer: _____
   _____

9. **What is the average weight (in pounds) of a fully grown elephant?**
   Answer: _____
   _____

10. **When and where did the game of tennis originate?**
    Answer: _____
    _____

Questions To Find Answers For, Page 2

11. How does a hydrofoil differ from a sailboat?
Answer: _____
_____

12. Where do koalas live and how do they look?
Answer: _____
_____

13. What use is a camel's hump to the camel?
Answer: _____
_____

14. Why is the rain forest so important to humanity?
Answer: _____
_____

15. Who was the first woman to win the Nobel Peace Prize?
Answer: _____
_____

16. What was the name of the American poet who wrote *The Song of Hiawatha*?
Answer: _____
_____

17. What makes ocean tides go in and out?
Answer: _____
_____

18. What is the tallest mountain range in the world and where is it located?
Answer: _____
_____

19. Who invented the zipper?
Answer: _____
_____

20. What causes tears?
Answer: _____
_____

Answers
To Write Questions For

Read the twenty answers below and write the best question you can for each answer.

1. Question:_____

_____

   Answer: Jonas Salk

2. Question:_____

_____

   Answer: Honduras

3. Question:_____

_____

   Answer: The Bermuda Triangle

4. Question:_____

_____

   Answer: Symmetry

5. Question:_____

_____

   Answer: Hang gliding

6. Question:_____

_____

   Answer: Illegal alien

7. Question:_____

_____

   Answer: Nuclear energy

8. Question:_____

_____

   Answer: Quadrilateral

9. Question:_____

_____

   Answer: Orangutan

10. Question:_____

_____

   Answer: Barrier Reef

Answers To Write Questions For, Page 2

11. Question:_____

_____

Answer: Venn Diagram

12. Question:_____

_____

Answer: Pharaoh

13. Question:_____

_____

Answer: Millennium

14. Question:_____

_____

Answer: Safari

15. Question:_____

_____

Answer: Pompeii

16. Question:_____

_____

Answer: Hieroglyphics

17. Question:_____

_____

Answer: Mozart

18. Question:_____

_____

Answer: Tyranny

19. Question:_____

_____

Answer: Onomatopoeia

20. Question:_____

_____

Answer: Anesthesiologist

An Introduction to the Cause and Effect Model for Solving Problems

Did you know that there are specific steps for solving a problem in the classroom to help students make decisions and find solutions in a more practical and efficient manner? The Cause and Effect Model helps students tackle problems on their own by illustrating how to identify the causes of a problem and then providing ways to evaluate the effects of the problem in order to arrive at the best possible solution.

1. Stating the Problem

This step requires the students to make a clear statement about the problem. The statement should be no more than two sentences in length.

2. Determining the Satisfaction Level

This step requires the students to assess what is happening that is unsatisfactory and what would be considered a satisfactory or acceptable level of performance.

3. Locating the Multiple Causes

This step requires the students to first identify all of the possible causes that are contributing to the unsatisfactory level of performance and then decide which of these causes are the most serious ones.

4. Considering Optional Solutions

This step requires the students to brainstorm for as many alternative solutions or proposed courses of action as possible, without making any evaluative judgments.

5. Establishing Solution Criteria

This step requires the students to establish a set of criteria and a scoring system to be used for evaluating each alternative solution proposed in Step Four.

6. Finding a Solution

This step requires the students to decide on a final course of action that is most likely to solve the problem using the criteria and scoring system established in Step Five.

Problems To Solve
Using the Cause and Effect Model

Background Information: The President of the United States has decided that students from distinguished schools throughout the country should serve on a Special Youth Advisory Board to help him or her deal with social, economic, and political issues in a more realistic manner. He or she has invited YOU to serve on this Advisory Board and to solve the most immediate set of problems outlined below. Work in a small group of 3 to 5 students to solve one of the problems using your own local school community as the locus of the problem situation.

PROBLEM OPTION ONE:

Sadly, today's urban centers have neglected to meet the physical fitness and recreational needs of its culturally diverse populations. Your task is to plan and design a park that will cover one square block and have something to offer people of all ages and ethnic backgrounds.

PROBLEM OPTION TWO:

A disproportionate number of young American families today are both hungry and homeless, with little encouragement or support for helping them to get out of their discouraging situation. Your task is to develop a blueprint for helping these citizens get back on their feet so that they can become more functional and productive in their everyday lives.

PROBLEM OPTION THREE:

A recent poll taken by the American public indicates that one major concern is the increase of street crime throughout lower, middle, and upper class neighborhoods. Your task is to plan a local community "anti-crime" campaign to reduce the anxiety and incidence of criminal activities in the area.

PROBLEM OPTION FOUR:

There is to be a "World's Fair for Fine Arts" in 1995. Each country who participates must create a sculpture which would be representative of its people and their corresponding lifestyle(s). You have been contracted to make a sculpture for the United States which would represent people of your generation. What will it look like?

PROBLEM OPTION FIVE:

You are on a committee which is to select a young person (either living or historical) to receive the coveted Nobel Award for Creativity. Your task is to serve on the panel that establishes criteria for the award, nominates at least five people who you feel are worthy of this great distinction, and then select the one person for the award, giving reasons for your choice.

Worksheet for Implementation of the Cause and Effect Model

GROUP MEMBERS

_____   _____

_____   _____

_____   _____

Problem Topic: _____

STATING THE PROBLEM:
Write down two complete sentences briefly describing the problem to be solved.

_____
_____
_____
_____
_____
_____
_____

DETERMINING THE SATISFACTION LEVEL:
Make a list of undesirable effects of the problem, and then make another list of desirable outcomes that would happen if the problem were solved.

_____
_____
_____
_____
_____
_____

LOCATING THE MULTIPLE CAUSES:
Write down all of the possible causes of the problem and place an asterisk (*) next to those items that represent the most likely causes of the problem.

_____
_____
_____
_____
_____

Worksheet for Implementation of the Cause and Effect Model, Page 2

CONSIDERING OPTIONAL SOLUTIONS:
Record all possible solutions or courses of action that one might take to solve the problem.

_____
_____
_____
_____
_____

ESTABLISHING SOLUTION CRITERIA:
Develop a set of criteria and a rating scale by which to evaluate the criteria and select the best solution for the problem.

_____
_____
_____
_____
_____

FINDING A SOLUTION:
Apply the criteria and rating scale to each of the possible solutions and decide which one best addresses your problem statement.

_____
_____
_____
_____
_____
_____

Tools
To Improve a Student's
Creative Thinking Skills

Did you know that there are several tools and techniques that you can use to look at "common things in uncommon ways"? For example, what might you do to an umbrella, a comb, or a toothbrush that would make it better and more effective or more efficient to use? Try applying several of these "verbs" or "actions" to one of the following objects in order to make it new and different: JUMP ROPE, FRISBEE, YO-YO, SKATEBOARD, or BASEBALL GLOVE. Write down your ideas and then draw your "improved" product!

SEPARATE: Take apart or break down into component parts.

_____

COMBINE: Add new parts or put old parts together in new and different ways.

_____

REDUCE: Make parts smaller in size.

_____

ENLARGE: Make parts larger in size.

_____

REARRANGE: Put parts together in different patterns or places.

_____

REVERSE: Put parts in an unusual sequence, format, or location.

_____

REVISE: Add new parts, remove parts, or substitute parts.

_____

CONVERT: Determine other tasks parts might be used for.

_____

Name _____

Using Math

READ

Ancient people measured length by comparing those things to be measured to body parts or sticks. Modern systems of measurement consist of standard units of measure. Therefore, rulers, yardsticks, and meter sticks are used throughout the world.

RELATE

Write a story entitled "A Day in the Life of a Meter Stick in a Seventh-Grade Math Class."

READ

A computer is an electronic device that performs calculations and processes information. The fastest computers are able to process millions of pieces of information in seconds.

RELATE

Tell how computers will change the roles of the teachers and the students in the 21st century.

READ

A clock is an instrument that shows the time. The first clocks were developed in the late 1200s. The word clock probably is related to the French word *cloche* and the German word *glocke,* both of which mean bell.

RELATE

React to this statement: A person's most precious resource is time.

READ

A thermometer is an instrument that measures the temperature of gases, liquids, and solids. Three types of thermometers include: liquid-in-glass, deformation-type, and electrical.

RELATE

Design an experiment using one of the three types of thermometers. Share your results.

Using Math, Page 2

READ

A protractor is used to measure angles. It has an inner scale and an outer scale. Place the center mark of the protractor on the vertex of an angle. Place the inner 0° mark on one side of the angle. Read the inner scale where the other side crosses the protractor.

RELATE

Formulate a poster showing at least ten other uses of a protractor. Include a precise description of each application.

READ

An instrument for drawing or measuring circles is a compass. It consists of two pointed branches joined at the top by a pivot.

RELATE

Use colored pencils in the compass to create several original overlapping circular designs to create a museum masterpiece. Write a feature article celebrating your work as if it were written by an art critic.

READ

A calculator performs mathematical operations with accuracy and speed. It has number buttons and command buttons. Some calculators show results in small display windows; some print out results.

RELATE

Imagine how it would be if your mind worked like a calculator; predict how your life might be made easier and how it might be made more complicated.

READ

A scale is a device used to measure weight. The four chief types of weighing scales are balance, spring, mechanical, and electronic.

RELATE

What might a scale say to each of the following: a fly, a newborn, a ton of bricks, and a set of weights?

Metrics

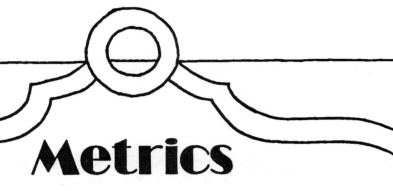

READ
Scientists and most other people throughout the world measure lengths, distances, weights, and other values by a standard method called the **metric system.**

RELATE
Pretend you are the editor of your local newspaper. Write an editorial about why metrics should or should not be taught in school.

READ
The metric system is based on units of 10. The principal unit is the **meter** which corresponds to the **yard** as a unit of length. The meter is 39.37 inches (1.093 yards).

RELATE
Pretend you are the unit "yard" and write a protest speech against your counterpart, the meter.

READ
The **liter** corresponds to the **quart** as a unit of capacity. It also has subdivisions and multiples of ten. One liter contains one cubic **decimeter** of liquid and one liter of water weighs one **kilogram.**

RELATE
Create a radio, newspaper, TV, or magazine advertisement for liter containers of your favorite soda. Be inventive. Present your advertisement to classmates.

READ
Prefixes are added to chief units:
deci = one-tenth   centi = one-hundredth   milli = one-thousandth

RELATE
Create a folktale whose main character is one decimeter tall. Tell about this character's lifestyle and relate some of his or her adventures.

Metrics, Page 2

READ

The basis of the metric system is the distance between the North Pole and the equator, which is about 6,200 miles. A line running from the North Pole to the equator can be divided into 10,000,000 equal parts; each part is a meter, or 39.37 inches.

RELATE

Write a travelogue about a trip on the imaginary line which runs from the North Pole to the equator.

READ

Scientists use the metric system to define physical and chemical constants, the "laws of nature." A spectrum is used to measure such microscopic distances as the diameter of an atom or electron.

RELATE

Discover other kinds of spectra. Name them. Describe them. What are their similarities? differences? Is there any kind of relationship among them? Explain.

READ

In 1866 Congress passed a law making the metric system legal in the United States for those who wish to use it. Some government departments, the armed forces, and NASA use the metric system.

RELATE

Prepare a series of arguments to debate whether or not Americans should be required to use only the metric system.

READ

A commission of French scientists developed the metric system in the 18th century. It has been revised several times, and in 1960 the present form was adopted and named the International System of Units, known as SI.

RELATE

Write a number autobiography using metric numbers. Include references for all important numbers in your life—heights, weights, shoe size, favorite radio station, address, distance to favorite restaurant, etc.

Mathematical Symbols

READ

The mathematical symbol for equality is =. This indicates that the number(s) on both sides of the symbol are equal. When both sides of an equation are not equal, the ≠ (does not equal) sign is used.

RELATE

Draw 10 symbols which relate to transportation. Use them as symbols in a rebus story about transportation.

READ

Symbols which indicate inequalities are as follows: < is less than and > is greater than. The symbol shows the relationship between the two sides of an equation.

RELATE

Write a comprehensive response to this question: How do you know if something is half full or half empty?

READ

In the field of geometry, symbols are used to show the relationship of figures. The term "is congruent to" is used instead of the term "equals." The symbol showing congruence is ≈; the symbol for incongruence is ≉.

RELATE

Design an imaginary figure using a rectangle and the symbols for equality, less and greater than, and incongruence. Name it, and tell what it does, where it lives, and how it contributes to society.

READ

Mathematical symbols showing arithmetic operations are + (addition), - (subtraction), x (multiplication), and ÷ (division).

RELATE

With a friend, compose an eight- to ten-line jingle about how important it is to know the four basic math operations.

Mathematical Symbols, Page 2

READ

A set is a collection of elements. Ancient people understood the concept of sets. In the 19th century, George Boole created symbols for sets. Set symbols include ($\in$) element, ($\ni$) not an element, ($\cup$) union, ($\cap$) intersection, and ($\subset$) subset.

RELATE

Write an explanation of why certain kids in your school are sometimes referred to by labels such as "jet set," "fashion set," "fast set," and "popular set."

READ

Symbols are used in the study of geometry to indicate ($\angle$) angle, ($\leftrightarrow$) line, ($\bigcirc$) circle, ($\mapsto$) line segment, ($\rightarrow$) ray, ($\perp$) perpendicular to, ($\parallel$) parallel to, and ($\triangle$) triangle.

RELATE

Use mathematical symbols to create a code of your own. Write a note to a friend using your new code.

READ

In the study of fractions, we deal with factors and multiples. Abbreviations associated with fractions include: LCM, least common multiple; GCF, greatest common factor; GCD, greatest common divisor.

RELATE

Associate these sets of letters with something else that is important to you. This will help you remember how these letters relate to fractions.

READ

One of two equal factors of a number is called its square root. (5 is the square root of 25 because 5 x 5 = 25). The symbol for square root is $\sqrt{}$ ($\sqrt{25} = 5$).

RELATE

Explain the following: square deal, square off, he's a square, square dance, square away, and square shooter.

Fractions

READ

Fractions written with one number above another are called "common" because that is the kind we usually see. This kind of fraction has been around for hundreds of years but is not always easy to work with. Decimals, for instance, are much easier to add and subtract.

RELATE

Suppose you are trying to convince the President of the United States that fractions should be replaced by decimals in all the schools in the country. What would you say about fractions and decimals to persuade the President that decimals are better?

READ

If a and b are whole numbers, $a \div b = \frac{a}{b}$ (remember, a is the numerator and b is the denominator).

RELATE

Imagine you have been changed into a number in a fraction. Which number are you, the numerator or denominator? Why did you choose to be this number?

READ

Christopher Rudolff, a German who lived in the 16th century, invented decimals to make the addition and subtraction of fractions easier.

RELATE

Imagine that you had invented decimals. How could you convince others that this method of adding and subtracting parts of a whole is simpler than using fractions?

READ

Unlike adding and subtracting, multiplying fractions is fairly easy. You simply multiply the numerators together and the denominators together.

RELATE

Create a kind of "association" saying which will help you and others remember and use the above information.

Fractions, Page 2

READ

To add fractions that have the same denominator, add the numerators. Use the common denominator. Then write the answer in lowest terms when necessary.

RELATE

If you were the math teacher, what could you do to illustrate the usefulness of changing the answer to its lowest terms?

READ

In order to add or subtract fractions, the denominators must be equal. You would change fractions such as ¼ and ⅓ into equivalent fractions with the same denominator and add the numerators to get the answer.

RELATE

Describe a funny situation in which the fraction ½ "refuses" to be transformed into an equivalent fraction in order to be added to ¾.

READ

Circles and pieces of circles are used to show that a fraction is part of a whole. For example, ¼ would look like this in a circle divided into 4 sections:

RELATE

Draw a circle and divide it into 8 sections. Label each section with the appropriate fraction. Then write a story about how it feels to be that fractional part of the whole.

READ

To find the lowest terms for a fraction a/b, divide a and b by their gcf (greatest common factor).

RELATE

Write about what you will do with all the extra time you have saved by knowing this math trick.

Nutrition

READ

Nutrition is the science that deals with foods and the way the body uses them. Good food is essential for health and survival. Food provides **nutrients** needed for good health.

RELATE

Create a class mascot who exemplifies perfect health. Name this mascot; draw and color. Record a history of its development.

READ

The body needs energy to maintain all its functions. The energy in food is measured in units called **food calories**. Everyone needs the same nutrients, but the amount needed varies from person to person.

RELATE

Create a series of alliterative statements about your favorite foods that are high in calories. Example: Perfect pizza pleases people and pacifies the palate.

READ

Nutritionists classify nutrients into five main groups: carbohydrates (starches and sugars in food), fats (fatty acids and glycerol), proteins (necessary for growth), minerals (essential for parts of bones and teeth), and vitamins (essential for good health).

RELATE

Write a name poem for each of the groups. Print the words vertically and complete the poem by using related words which include each letter.

Example:
```
Fatty
mArgarine
buTter
greaSe
```

READ

There are two different ways of categorizing the foods we need to eat for good health: the **Basic Seven Food Group** and the **Basic Four Food Group**. The Basic Four consists of a milk, a meat, a bread and cereal, and a fruit and vegetable group.

RELATE

Research to find out about the Basic Seven Food Group and create a chart of both the Basic Seven and the Basic Four.

Nutrition, Page 2

READ

Malnutrition is caused by not eating enough food or by not eating foods with enough nutrients. Starvation is extreme undernutrition.

RELATE

Invite a guest speaker to talk to your class about anorexia, bulimia, and other related diseases. Write a series of interview questions you would like to ask him or her.

READ

Vitamin deficiencies are caused by a lack of vitamins in the diet. Symptoms vary. Vitamin D deficiency, called **rickets,** causes abnormal development of the bones.

RELATE

Create a photoessay from newspaper and magazine pictures showing people who suffer from nutritional deficiencies.

READ

A diet high in salt may result in high blood pressure, or hypertension. This increases the risk of heart attack and stroke.

RELATE

Write a jingle warning about the correlation between salt and hypertension. Perform your jingle for your class.

READ

Vocations related to nutrition include medicine, chemistry, home economics, and agricultural research. Nutritionist research has helped reduce hunger throughout the world, but malnutrition still exists and is an important world problem.

RELATE

Write a persuasive paragraph explaining why you would or would not like to be a health care worker when out of school.

Endangered Species

READ

The Bald Eagle is the emblem of the United States. Its picture is on coins and dollar bills. It is protected by law but is dying out and may soon be extinct because of pollution and firearms.

RELATE

Write a funny story about a Bald Eagle who needed a haircut.

READ

A large Grizzly Bear may be 4½ feet high at the shoulders and weigh as much as 900 pounds. If it stands up on its rear legs, it may reach eight or nine feet! It usually fishes by wading into a stream and snatching up a fish in its mouth.

RELATE

Write your version of the "Hug Therapy Book."

READ

The Kit Fox is the smallest of all North American foxes. It is not much bigger than a kitten. The Kit Fox lives in deserts and prairies, hunts for meat to eat at night, and sleeps during the day.

RELATE

Create a play in which a family adopts a Kit Fox, thinking it is a baby Siamese cat.

READ

The Whooping Crane is the tallest bird in North America. It lives in a tiny marshy place on the coast of Texas in the winter and in the spring flies to northern Canada. The Crane has long legs and wades in water to look for food.

RELATE

You've heard of a "bird's eye view." Tell about some things the Whooping Crane might see on his migratory flight from Texas to Canada.

Endangered Species, Page 2

READ

The California Condor is one of the largest flying birds in the world. It once lived in most of western North America, but now those that are left live in a sanctuary in southern California. When outstretched, its wings measure more than nine feet from tip to tip.

RELATE

Tell a story about a condor who hated his life in the sanctuary because it restricted his freedom.

READ

The Texas Ocelot is sometimes called a leopard cat. It has spots and rings like a leopard and short stripes like a tiger. It is about twice as big as a house cat. Today it is found only in small areas of Texas and Mexico.

RELATE

Draw the Texas Ocelot from the description above. Create a limerick to go with your drawing.

READ

The Sea Otter is a marine animal that inhabits the coastal waters of the Pacific Ocean from northern California to northern Alaska. Its two hind feet are long flippers. Its fur is made up of two layers which keep the Otter warm and relatively dry.

RELATE

Create a story line for a pilot show for a series about a friendly Sea Otter.

READ

The Florida Panther is the last of the big cats east of the Mississippi River. It probably numbers fewer than 50 today, and is found mainly in the remote Everglades of Florida.

RELATE

Create an acceptance speech for a panther who has just been named to the Florida's Animal Hall of Fame.

Climate

READ

Climate includes temperature, wind, sunshine, humidity, and rainfall. The study of climate is called **climatology.** A location's variety of weather conditions can be called **climate** if the conditions endure for many years.

RELATE

Formulate as many words as possible from the letters in the word CLIMATOLOGY. Use these to write a series of riddles related to the weather.

READ

Climate affects our way of life, the clothing we wear, the kinds of food we raise, the kinds of houses we live in, and the kinds of transportation we use.

RELATE

In what ways does the climate where you live affect what you wear, what you eat, and how you live? Compose a skit to show the effects of the climate on your lifestyle.

READ

Climate creates patterns of hot, cold, dry, and rainy regions throughout the world. The cold regions are near the poles; the warm regions are near the equator. The climate of any large region may vary greatly.

RELATE

Find a poem you like about the weather. Illustrate it using crayons, markers, or watercolors. Display your poem with your drawing.

READ

Latitude affects climate in two ways: the height of the noon sun and the length of the day. These factors determine the amount of heat received from the sun.

RELATE

Write a science fiction short story entitled "When the Earth's Axis Slipped."

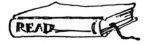 

Climate, Page 2

READ

Man is able to change the climate in a small area. Rainfall can be increased by seeding clouds with dry ice. When cities are built, forests destroyed, or crops planted in a barren field, man can change the climate.

RELATE

Find evidence to support the hypothesis that man is adversely changing the climate. Write an editorial to convince others that this problem exists.

READ

Portuguese explorers sailing far south along the west coast of Africa found people living in regions at the equator. Other explorers such as Columbus, Drake, and Magellan extended the knowledge of climate in regions far from Europe.

RELATE

Create a series of mock headlines to show the discoveries of the Portuguese. Use one of these to develop a news story or feature story for a newspaper.

READ

Scientists developed the thermometer, barometer, and wind gauge in the 1500s and 1600s. These instruments measured certain conditions of the air and helped scientists study climate and weather.

RELATE

If you could be a weather instrument, which one would you be and why?

READ

Today, new knowledge of the upper atmosphere (thanks to high-altitude balloons, space rockets, and artificial satellites) indicates that changes in climate may be related to changes in the sun's radiation.

RELATE

Record what it must be like to soar through the sky as a balloon, a rocket, or a satellite.

 © 1994 by Incentive Publications, Inc., Nashville, TN.

Government

READ
Every group of people has rules of conduct which govern the lives of its members. Most rules relate to acceptable and unacceptable kinds of behavior. Most persons obey these rules.

RELATE
Write and illustrate 5 to 10 rules of conduct for one or more of the following:
a school of fish   a covey of quail   a den of lions   a herd of elephants

READ
The basic set of laws by which a people is governed is called a constitution. The U.S. Constitution is the oldest written national constitution still in force. It lists the rights and liberties of the American people.

RELATE
Imagine how you would feel if the rights and liberties granted you by the Constitution were taken from you. Explain your feelings. How might your life be changed?

READ
The U.S. Constitution provides for a government with these three separate branches: (1) the executive, represented by the President; (2) the legislative, represented by Congress; and (3) the judicial, represented by the Supreme Court.

RELATE
Develop a campaign platform, slogan, and speech advocating a teenage President of the United States.

READ
A private government rules only the members of a particular group; a public government rules all the individuals and groups within a certain geographical area.

RELATE
Write a letter to the President of the U.S. telling him or her you think there is too much drug abuse among young people today and what both private and public sectors can do about it.

Government, Page 2

READ

An amendment is a change made in a law, a constitution, or a legislative bill. The first 10 amendments, known as the Bill of Rights, were proposed on September 25, 1789.

RELATE

Create a Bill of Rights for a group of endangered species.

READ

The Bill of Rights is a document that describes the basic liberties of the people and forbids the government to violate those rights. The U.S. Bill of Rights consists of the first 10 amendments to the Constitution.

RELATE

Devise a "Student Bill of Rights" for your school. Share with your teacher and classmates.

READ

In the United States, government service is a major field of employment. It offers a wide variety of well-paid jobs that attract men and women from almost every occupation.

RELATE

Work in groups of 3 to 5 to create a "Career Catalog of Jobs in Government."

READ

The democratic idea of government is that the government serves the people. The Communist idea is that the people serve the government.

RELATE

With a partner, debate the merits of these two conflicting forms of government. Does each have merits and disadvantages?

Islands

READ

An island is any body of land smaller than a continent and completely surrounded by water. Islands may be floating, oceanic, continental, inland, or land-tied.

RELATE

If you were on a desert island with only one other person, who would it be and why? Write a paragraph discussing this situation.

READ

Greenland is the largest island in the world. Its size is 840,000 square miles. Seven-eighths of it is covered with ice, and the northern tip is about 440 miles from the North Pole.

RELATE

Develop a travel brochure for Greenland. Include factual information and illustrations.

READ

Islands are homes for some people and vacation spots for others. Some islands are used for defense, for storing fuels and supplies for aircraft and ships, and for protecting trade routes.

RELATE

Write a travel tip article for people who are planning a vacation to a new place called Cloud Island.

READ

New Guinea is the second largest island in the world. It has the highest mountains of any island and is covered with wild, thick jungles.

RELATE

Pretend you are a mountain climber who has just reached the top of the highest mountain in New Guinea. Give an interview to the local reporters.

Islands, Page 2

READ
Hawaiian islands are considered oceanic islands. These islands lie in the open ocean far from any continent. They are formed of coral or volcanic lava.

RELATE
Write an essay of at least three paragraphs on "Why I Do (or Don't) Want To Visit Hawaii."

READ
Floating islands on inland waters can be made of masses of earth and driftwood. The Chinese build floating islands to serve as foundations for gardens.

RELATE
If you could build a floating island, where would you build it, what would you use to build it, and what would you use it for?

READ
Australia is sometimes classified as an island as well as a continent and a country. It is larger than Greenland. It has the sixth largest area in the world.

RELATE
Write a fairy tale or legend about a kangaroo and/or a koala. Present this to your class.

READ
Japan is an island country in the Pacific Ocean. Four large islands and many smaller ones make up Japan. If the four large islands were placed along the eastern coast of the United States, they would extend from Maine to Florida.

RELATE
Create a stained glass window depicting the beauty of Japan. Write a narrative to explain it.

Justice

READ
The Department of Justice is an executive department of the United States government. The Attorney General heads the department, which enforces federal laws and provides legal advice for the President.

RELATE
Write a newspaper editorial giving your point of view about the criminal justice system in the United States.

READ
The Attorney General is appointed by the President with Senate approval. He or she acts as the chief legal officer of the federal government.

RELATE
Design a greeting card for the Attorney General of the United States. Write a brief message, illustrate, sign, and send.

READ
Definitions of justice: (1) a judge of the Supreme Court of the U.S.; (2) maintenance of just treatment; (3) that which is merited or due with regards to standards of what is fair, upright, or moral.

RELATE
Outline a story for an episode of "People's Court" or some other court-related program.

READ
The Supreme Court of the United States is the highest court in the nation. One of its basic duties is to determine whether federal, state, and local governments are acting according to the U.S. Constitution.

RELATE
Redesign the robe worn by the justices of the Supreme Court. Write a fashion article describing how it has influenced new night-time wear for the public.

Justice, Page 2

READ

The Supreme Court has nine members, a chief justice, and eight associate justices. The exact number is determined by Congress and has changed through the years.

RELATE

Create a story plot in which a chief justice has nine lives.

READ

One of the most famous of all American judges, John Marshall, wrote many of the most important and historic Supreme Court opinions when he served as chief justice from 1801 to 1835.

RELATE

Rewrite a famous court case of your choosing with a different outcome or ending.

READ

The Court of Appeals is a high federal or state court. The U.S. Court of Appeals ranks next to the Supreme Court as a reviewing authority. The Court of Appeals divides its work into 10 judicial circuits.

RELATE

Have you ever wished that you could be heard before a Court of Appeals? For what reason? Relate the circumstances.

READ

In the early days in the United States, federal judges traveled from place to place to try cases and to hear appeals. The route which was assigned was called a circuit. Today the circuits are geographical areas. The eleventh circuit covers only the District of Columbia.

RELATE

Pretend you are a circuit court judge in some rural area of the United States. Keep a log of your cases and their outcomes.

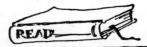 

Poetry

READ

Poetry is defined as a rich, colorful way of speaking and writing. The three main kinds of poetry are **lyric, narrative,** and **dramatic.**

RELATE

Select a famous poem to perform as a choral reading in your class. Assign parts, practice, and have fun.

READ

Lyric poetry is the most common type of poetry and is usually short. **Haiku,** a Japanese lyric form, consists of 17 syllables arranged in three lines of 5, 7, 5 syllables. Haiku usually relates to an element of nature and appeals to one or more of the senses.

RELATE

Write and illustrate your own personal haiku poem.

READ

Two other types of lyric poems are the ode and the elegy. An **ode** is a serious, elaborate poem full of high praise and noble feeling. An **elegy** is a meditation on life and death.

RELATE

Have you read an ode or an elegy? Share your impressions. Compose two original titles, one for an ode and one for an elegy.

READ

Narrative poems tell stories. The two chief types are **epics** and **ballads.** Epics are long poems that describe heroic deeds or tell the history of a people. Epics are probably the oldest surviving form of poetry.

RELATE

Read an epic poem suggested by your teacher. Summarize it.

Poetry, Page 2

READ

A **ballad** tells a story, usually about a specific person. For example, many English ballads describe the adventures of Robin Hood, a legendary outlaw who robbed the rich to give to the poor.

RELATE

Write an original ballad based on a superhero (real or imaginary).

READ

A **limerick** is a five-line form of humorous verse. It consists of 13 beats and has a rhyme scheme in the pattern **aabba.**

RELATE

Search for a limerick you enjoy. Read it, copy it onto posterboard, and illustrate it. Try creating a few limericks of your own.

READ

Two kinds of comparisons in poetry are **simile** and **metaphor.** Two unlike things are compared using **like** or **as** in a simile (your eyes are **like** blue pools). A metaphor states that something is something else (your eyes **are** blue pools).

RELATE

Find at least three examples of each kind of comparison. Illustrate all; have classmates guess what the comparisons are. Write three original comparisons of your own.

READ

Two very famous poets are William Shakespeare (England) and Edgar Allan Poe (United States). Another famous American poet is Robert Frost.

RELATE

Who is your favorite poet? Why? Design a trophy, certificate, or ribbon for this person. Create a fact sheet about him or her.

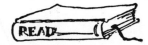

Word Etymologies

READ

Here is the dictionary entry for **dessert.**

dessert (dĭ-zûrt´) n. course served at the end of a meal, usually a sweet food. [French dessert, from desservir to clear the table, going back to Latin: des-, away + servire, to serve].

RELATE

Identify your favorite dessert. Describe how it looks and how it tastes. How often do you enjoy this dessert and why is it your favorite?

READ

Here is the etymology for **sleep.**

[Old English slœpan to slumber, be dead, be numb, be inert.]

RELATE

Retell a favorite bedtime story from your early childhood, using slang terms and up-to-date language. How does it change the flavor?

READ

When a word has an interesting history, information about its origin is provided in the form of an anecdote also in brackets at the end of the dictionary entry.

RELATE

Discover the anecdotes for **boycott, sandwich,** and **clerk.** Which one was your favorite and why?

READ

Etymology is derived from the French, from Latin, and from Greek, all meanings related to **origin.**

RELATE

Imagine our alphabet without the letters **e** and **s.** What words would you miss the most and why?

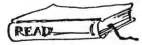 

Word Etymologies, Page 2

READ

Etymology is the study of the history and development of words. It concerns the origin of words and the way their meanings and spelling have changed throughout the years.

RELATE

Create a new word to add to the English language. Write its pronunciation, part of speech, meaning, sample sentence, and etymology. Illustrate if you wish.

READ

Cognates are words which come from a common origin. For example, catch and chase come from the Latin word *captare*.

RELATE

Write a one-page anecdote which includes the words catch, chase, and capture.

READ

English history reflects the growth of English words. Saxons provided the foundation; Romans, Danes, and Norman French later provided many of their own words in the English language.

RELATE

How many definitions/synonyms can you come up with for the word **run**? How does your list compare to the one in the dictionary? Use five of your words in a compound or complex sentence.

READ

Most dictionaries will provide information on the etymology (derivation) of many of the entry words. Usually this information is placed in brackets [ ] at the end of the dictionary entry.

RELATE

Invent a character which represents brackets. Name him, color him, and have some fun using him.

Newspapers

READ

Newspapers are publications which are devoted to presenting current news and commenting upon the news and related events.

RELATE

Draw a political cartoon for your local paper.

READ

Daily, Sunday, weekly, and bi-weekly newspapers are an important part of home life in most American families. News stories tell of local, state, national, and international happenings.

RELATE

Create a trivia game using facts found in your daily newspaper. Play it with your classmates.

READ

Daily newspapers include news stories, sports, society, finance, agriculture, religion, education, editorial comments, features, obituaries, comics, and advertising.

RELATE

You want to start a school newspaper. Outline the types of articles you would want to include and complete one as a sample to share with your teacher.

READ

Large city newspapers have many employees who are organized into staffs, headed by a publisher, with editorial, business, and mechanical departments.

RELATE

Discover the qualifications you need to become a newspaper carrier for a local publication. Write a want ad to recruit carriers.

Newspapers, Page 2

READ

An "eXtra" is an edition of a newspaper published at a time other than a scheduled regular edition. The "banner" is the top headline on page one and, in an "eXtra," is most important.

RELATE

Write a special edition of a day's headline news designed just for kids.

READ

The first newspaper is considered to be *Tsing Pao,* which was a court journal published in Peking. It started in the 500s and was continued until 1935.

RELATE

Speculate on what you think the first newspaper was like, based on the Asian culture it represented.

READ

The first daily newspaper in England was the *London Daily Courant,* begun in 1702 by a woman, Elizabeth Mallett.

RELATE

Develop an award or certificate for a specialized news story. Select three articles from your local newspaper you feel deserve the award or certificate of merit and explain why.

READ

The "Penny Papers" were started in the 1830s. They were very large in page size, sold for six cents, and were very popular with the public.

RELATE

Compare and contrast TV news with printed news. Which do you prefer? Why?

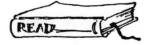

MAKING SURE THEY ARE TAUGHT— NOT CAUGHT— IN THE MIDDLE

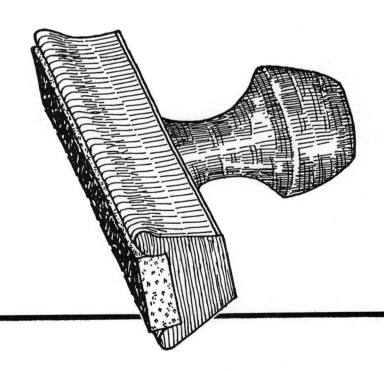

Taking a Personal Look at Interdisciplinary Instruction (Agree or Disagree Statements)

On a rating scale of 1 to 5, indicate whether you agree or disagree with each of these statements about integration of subject matter. Use the following benchmarks to help you make your decision. Try to give one good reason for your rating for each situation.

1 = I do not agree with this statement at all.
3 = I agree somewhat with this statement.
5 = I fully agree with this statement.

___ **Statement One:** There should be a single definition of interdisciplinary instruction so that all teachers have a common understanding of what it is and what it is not.

Reason: _____

_____

_____

___ **Statement Two:** Interdisciplinary units should follow a standard format and cover a specific period or amount of time to ensure continuity of the curriculum.

Reason: _____

_____

_____

___ **Statement Three:** Interdisciplinary instruction ought to be the major focus of both interdisciplinary teaming and interdisciplinary team meetings.

Reason: _____

_____

_____

___ **Statement Four:** Interdisciplinary units represent the best delivery system for teaching content and skills to students because students do best when learning is connected.

Reason: _____

_____

_____

___ **Statement Five:** It is easier to find time for planning, implementing, and evaluating interdisciplinary units than it is for teaching subjects and skills in isolated content areas during a typical school day, week, month, or year.

Reason: _____

_____

_____

Self-Check List of Steps toward Integration of Subject Matter

Put a check mark next to each of the following steps that you have tried with your team members when beginning to integrate the disciplines.

___ **Step One:** Our team has reached consensus on a workable definition of interdisciplinary instruction for our use during this school year.

___ **Step Two:** Our team held a brainstorming session to determine common themes, topics, skills, concepts, and timelines that might lend themselves to an interdisciplinary unit for our students. We used a planning matrix for this purpose recording our overlapping topics, skills, and concepts for each month of the school year.

___ **Step Three:** Our team conducted a formal team meeting and selected one major theme from the information on the matrix that had special relevance to all team members and their respective subject areas. We then brainstormed a large number of related topics for one another's subject areas.

___ **Step Four:** Each member of our team went on a treasure hunt and collected a wide variety of resource materials on the theme from the school and community libraries. We also gathered a number of activities that were content specific in each of our disciplines.

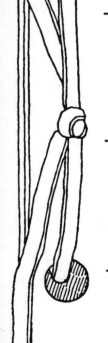

___ **Step Five:** Each member of our team prepared an outline for teaching the interdisciplinary theme agreed upon in Step Three that included the key skills or concepts that were going to be important parts of the interdisciplinary process in his or her content area. These were shared among team members so that similarities and differences could be noted and coordinated among us.

___ **Step Six:** We all exchanged classes for at least one period, teaching one another's subject areas according to a prepared lesson plan. This gave us an opportunity to work in another discipline and the students an opportunity to see us as teachers in another area.

___ **Step Seven:** We all designed a set of lesson plans in our own discipline for one week that did not use the textbook as a delivery system, but rather included a variety of different instructional strategies to give us practice in writing our own "interdisciplinary" set of tasks.

___ **Step Eight:** We also decided upon an individual skill and/or concept (such as making inferences and/or interdependence) and developed a short series of lesson plans to teach that skill/concept in each of our disciplines for an entire week.

___ **Step Nine:** We held a set of consecutive team meetings to sit down and plan our mutual interdisciplinary unit around the established theme. Our plan included a commonly agreed upon set of content and skill objectives, a glossary of terms, an information sheet of background information on the theme for the students, a collection of related activities for each discipline, a set of final project options, and a bibliography.

___ **Step Ten:** We composed a letter to parents and guardians informing them of our upcoming interdisciplinary unit and inviting them to become involved in a variety of ways.

The Interdisciplinary Web as a Planning Tool for Teachers

An Interdisciplinary Web is an excellent strategy for helping teachers on a team plan an interdisciplinary unit. To begin this process, the team agrees on a common theme or topic and writes this in the center of a large piece of paper. Moving from the center outwards, related ideas or subtopics are recorded to begin to form the web. Additional levels of subtopics can be added in like manner to form several levels of related skills and concepts until the final product looks much like the web of a spider. An example of an Interdisciplinary Web is illustrated below. A blank web is included on the next page so that you and your team members can practice this webbing process on a topic of your own choosing.

WEBBING

Webbing is an open-ended planning process which allows teachers to see relationships between ideas and subject/skill areas. The webbing process is a tool that assists teachers in generating ideas which might be lost in more traditional planning techniques.

1. Write the topic to be explored in the center of a circle drawn on a chalkboard or chart paper.
2. Brainstorm in a free association manner.

Interdisciplinary Web

As an interdisciplinary team, take a few minutes to fill in the blank web below using a topic or theme of your own choice. Instead of writing just words or phrases for each subtopic of the web, you might want to try writing a series of related questions or tasks in each space. An example (related to the Interdisciplinary Web model on the previous page) might be:

How do sounds differ in pitch?
1. Listen to a tape of animal sounds.
2. Attend a performance of a symphony or band.
3. Set up "glass" experiment to vary pitch through volume of water contained in a set of glasses.

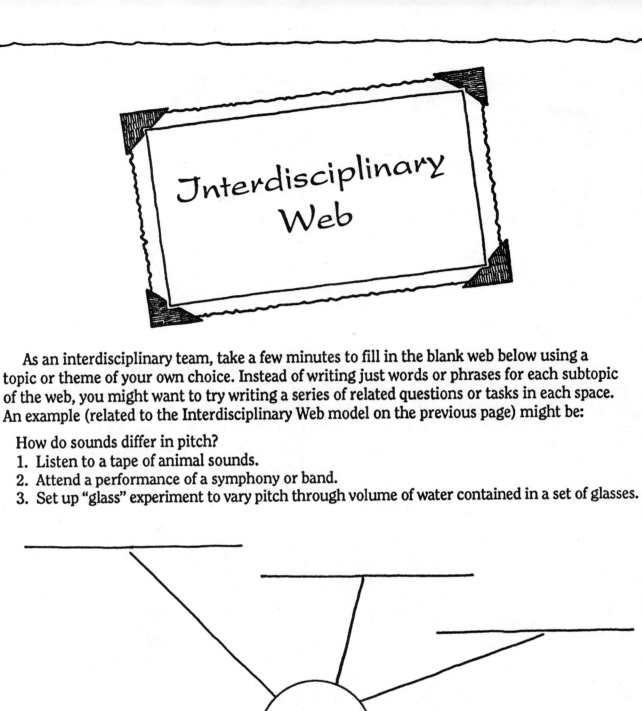

The Interdisciplinary Tree as a Planning Tool for Teachers

An Interdisciplinary Tree is a reproduction or outline of a tree with a trunk and a set of roots, branches, and leaves. A team of teachers uses this tree facsimile to record their ideas for an interdisciplinary unit by writing the theme or topic on the trunk, the material resources on the roots, the concepts on the branches, and the related skills on the leaves. An example of a completed Interdisciplinary Tree for a unit on CHOCOLATE appears below. A blank Interdisciplinary Tree is included on page 189 for you to fill out as a team with a topic of your choice.

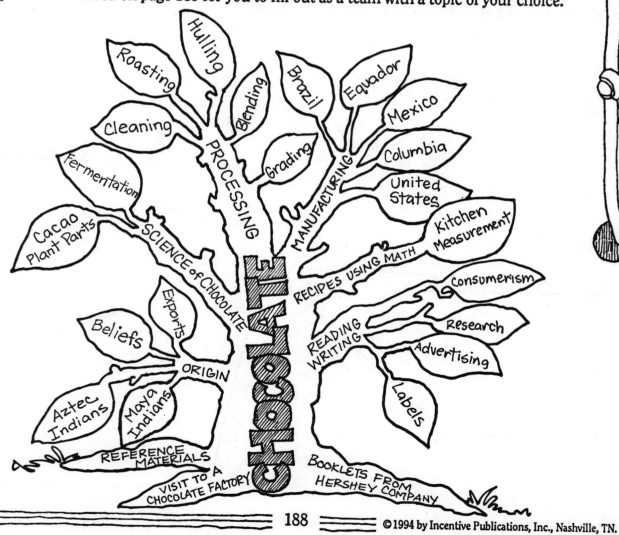

Interdisciplinary Tree

Use the Interdisciplinary Tree outline below to plan your own integrated unit on a topic of your choice. Record your overall theme or topic on the trunk, your material resources on the roots, your subject matter concepts on the branches, and your related skills on the leaves.

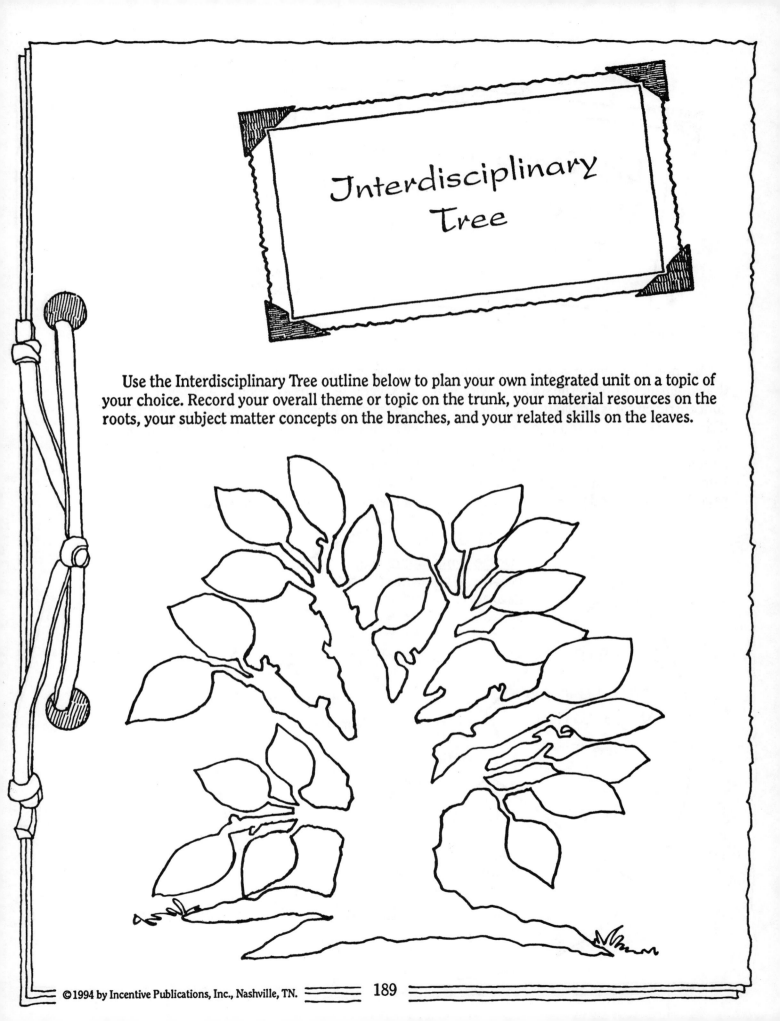

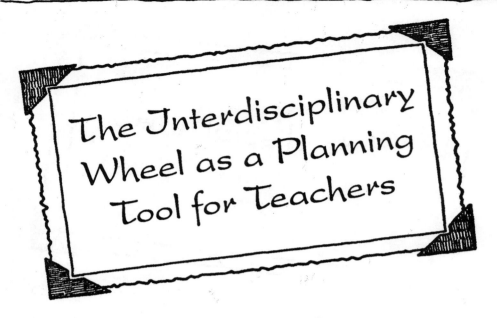

The Interdisciplinary Wheel as a Planning Tool for Teachers

An Interdisciplinary Wheel is constructed by drawing a large circle on a big piece of drawing paper or posterboard and dividing it into several sections or wedges. A smaller concentric circle is drawn in the center of the large circle. It contains the name of the interdisciplinary theme or topic to be studied. Related topics, concepts, skills, and/or activities are recorded within the appropriate wedges so that one can tell at a glance what the primary content, tasks, and resources will be for this interdisciplinary unit of instruction. A sample Interdisciplinary Wheel is completed below. A blank Interdisciplinary Wheel is available on page 191 for you and your team to complete on a theme or topic of your choice.

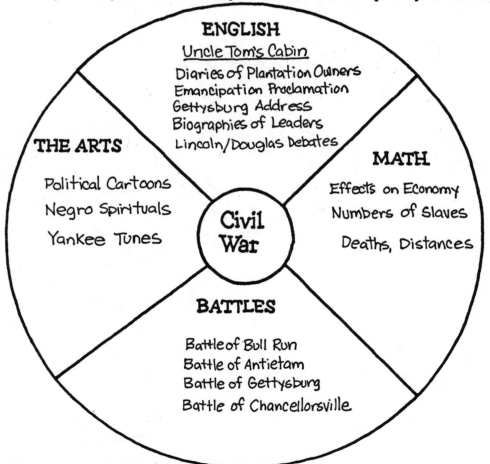

ENGLISH
Uncle Tom's Cabin
Diaries of Plantation Owners
Emancipation Proclamation
Gettysburg Address
Biographies of Leaders
Lincoln/Douglas Debates

MATH
Effects on Economy
Numbers of Slaves
Deaths, Distances

BATTLES
Battle of Bull Run
Battle of Antietam
Battle of Gettysburg
Battle of Chancellorsville

THE ARTS
Political Cartoons
Negro Spirituals
Yankee Tunes

Civil War

Interdisciplinary Wheel

Use the Interdisciplinary Wheel below as a tool for planning an interdisciplinary unit on a special theme or topic of interest to you and your students. Write the name of the unit in the smaller circle and place the subtopics, anticipated resources, and prescribed activities along the circumference of the larger circle within the designated wedges.

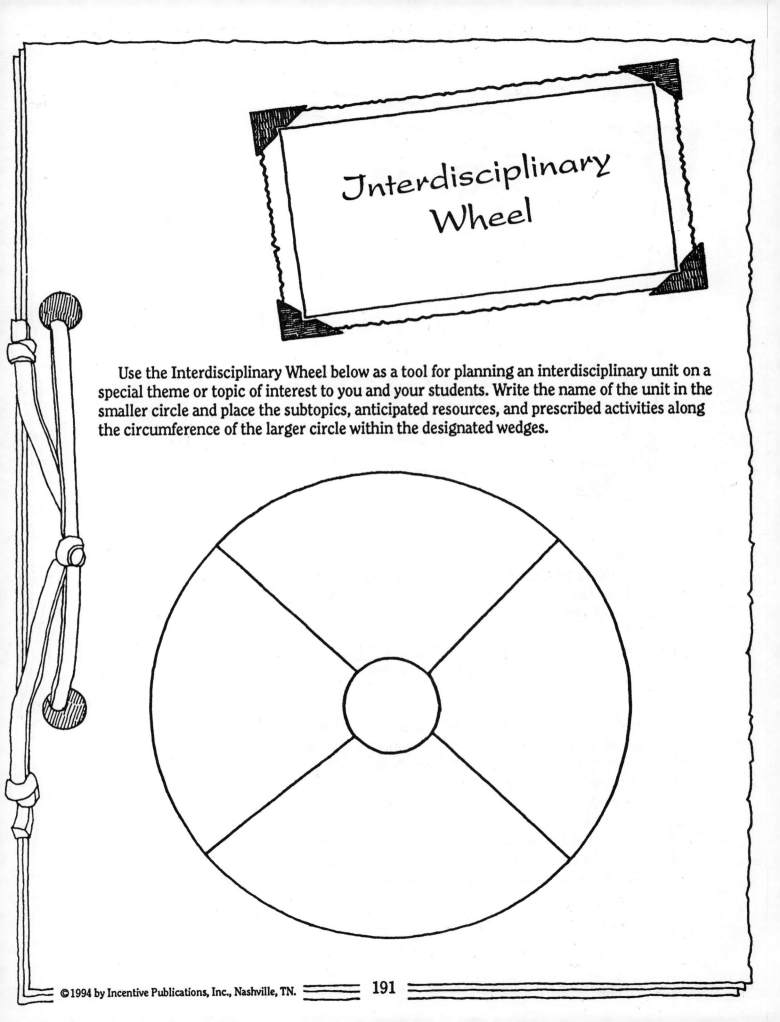

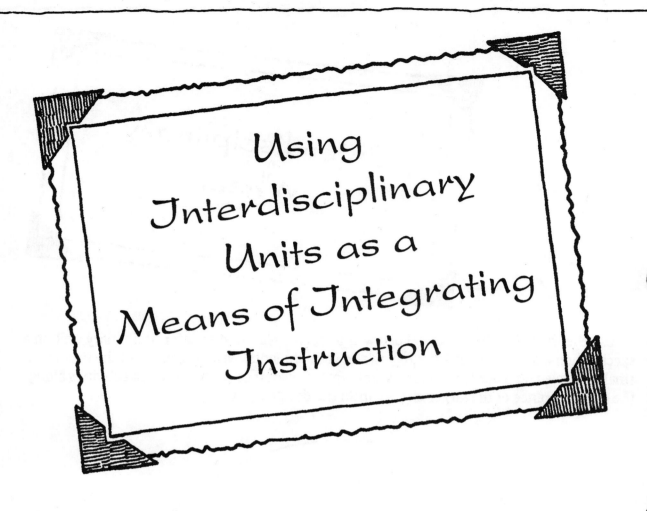

Using Interdisciplinary Units as a Means of Integrating Instruction

Interdisciplinary units are perhaps the most widely used and most effective approach to organizing and presenting information and concepts drawn from a combination of subject areas in a connected and coherent manner. The selection of a theme of high interest to students provides for curriculum integration, reduces fragmentation and repetition of content and skills, facilitates the development of thinking and study skills, and reinforces interpersonal and social skills.

Mini-units planned to be presented over a period usually ranging from three to seven days are often developed to teach or reinforce specific skills, concepts, and understandings. These units generally require less preparation time for the teacher, fewer materials, and consume a smaller block of instructional time. Follow-up activities are important components of these units since one of their major purposes is to stimulate interest in the subject and arouse curiosity for further exploration. It is of the utmost importance, then, that the objectives, information, and directions be clear, concise, and complete. The model unit "Pablo Picasso, His Life and Work" has been developed as an example of this type of mini-unit.

One-day mini-mini units comprised of quick-and-easy but challenging activities related to one specific and closely contained subject may be developed to add interest and excitement to the daily routine. The integration of different subject areas in this manner enables the student to approach the knowledge base as a whole rather than in piecemeal fashion and to achieve a more compact understanding of the chosen subject. One very effective organizational approach to the mini-mini unit is through the use of Bloom's Taxonomy of Cognitive Thinking Skills. The one-day units, "Japan," "Uranium," and "Weight," provide examples of mini-mini-units with a science theme, a social studies theme, and a math theme.

The model outline for an interdisciplinary unit on page 194 may be used in its entirety to design an extended unit to be presented over several weeks' time or a shorter, more concise unit consisting of the same basic elements but comprised of fewer student activities. Individual teachers and/or team members planning together may choose to add, subtract, or substitute components to better suit the unique needs of their students. It is important, however, to retain the basic elements in order to present separate content subjects in a truly integrated manner. A complete extended interdisciplinary unit with a language arts focus, "The Magic and Mystery of Messages," has been included as an example.

All five of the model units are ready to be reproduced for classroom use:

Outline for an
Interdisciplinary Mini-Unit

Title: _____
_____

Theme: _____
_____
_____

Objective: _____
_____

Information: _____
_____
_____
_____
_____

Introductory Activity: _____
_____
_____

Language Arts: _____
_____
_____

Math: _____
_____
_____

Science: _____
_____
_____

Social Studies: _____
_____
_____

Culminating Activity: _____
_____
_____

Follow-up Activities: _____
_____
_____

Pablo Picasso, His Life and Work

Sample One-Week Interdisciplinary Unit

Objective:
To learn more about the life and work of Pablo Picasso.

Information:
Pablo Ruiz y Picasso was born in 1881 in Málaga, Spain. He was a painter and a sculptor who was influenced by the Impressionist movement at the beginning of his career. His early pictures were done mainly in blue and portrayed the poverty he saw in Spain. Later, he moved to Paris and studied and worked with Georges Braque in a style known as Cubism. He painted pictures showing figures as fragments of geometric shapes. During the Spanish Civil War, he became deeply involved in politics. One of Picasso's most famous pictures is *Guernica*, which shows the destruction of a Spanish town. Picasso's work was suppressed by the Nazis during World War II. Picasso died in southern France in 1973. He may be the best-known 20th-century painter. His work has greatly influenced other painters.

Introduction:
Review some of Picasso's paintings in books from the media center. Note the features and qualities unique to his paintings. Review the facts of his life and determine the influence of his life experiences on his work.

LANGUAGE ARTS

Write a friendly letter to Picasso telling him why you do or do not like his paintings. What artistic advice would you give him if he were able to paint in the 1990s?

MATH

Why is measurement and proportion important to an artist? Explain your answer.

SCIENCE

What is the chemical makeup of paint that artists use? Find out about differences in paint—watercolors, oils, acrylics, etc. Share your information verbally with the class.

CULMINATING ACTIVITY

Read in an encyclopedia about the life of Picasso. Share your information with the class by performing a "living biography." Dress as Picasso did and share five to ten facts about his life. You should "become" Picasso—really feel the part.

FOLLOW-UP ACTIVITIES

. . . Try to find out how much Picasso's paintings are sold for now and where some of his best-known works are located. Find out if the demand for his work and the price of the paintings have increased or decreased since his death.

. . . Use reference books to find out more about Picasso's life. Write a short biography, summarizing the important stages and events in his life.

. . . Study Picasso's use of line and color and experiment with paints or colored chalk to express yourself "Picasso style."

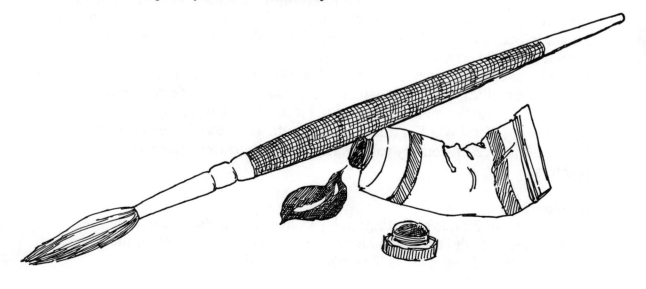

Outline for a Mini-Mini-Unit Using Bloom's Taxonomy of Cognitive Thinking Skills

Title: _____

Theme: _____
_____

Objective: _____
_____

Knowledge: _____
_____
_____
_____

Application: _____
_____
_____
_____

Synthesis: _____
_____
_____
_____

Comprehension: _____
_____
_____
_____

Analysis: _____
_____
_____

Evaluation: _____
_____
_____
_____

JAPAN

KNOWLEDGE:
Locate Japan on a world map. Count the main islands which make up this country. Name the capital. Identify Japan's latitude and longitude.

COMPREHENSION:
Give examples of major Japanese imports and exports.

SYNTHESIS:
Design a new Japanese flag to reflect both its history and its Eastern and Western cultures. Color and display.

APPLICATION:
Construct a relief map of Japan. Be sure to include a key. Locate the capital and major cities. Display.

EVALUATION:
Consider the portrayal of Japan in a movie you have seen or a book you have read. Was this country portrayed in a positive or negative light? Defend your answer.

ANALYSIS:
Examine Japan's history to see how it has influenced its art forms.

198

URANIUM

COMPREHENSION:
Explain <u>radioactive dating</u> to find the age of igneous rock. Determine the difference between nuclear fission and nuclear fusion.

KNOWLEDGE:
Locate the meaning and the etymology of <u>uranium</u>. State uranium's chief use.

ANALYSIS:
Discover the properties of uranium and the three isotopes of uranium.

APPLICATION:
Locate on a world map the areas of major known uranium deposits and make generalizations related to your findings.

EVALUATION:
Justify the use of nuclear energy to solve the major energy problems of the world.

SYNTHESIS:
Imagine a world without uranium. How would our history and our life as we know it today be different?

WEIGHT

ANALYSIS: Compare and contrast the metric and the standard units of measure. Identify the advantages and disadvantages of each.

COMPREHENSION: Determine which standard unit _and_ which metric unit you would use to measure each of these:
- your weight
- a letter
- a sack of potatoes
- a loaf of bread
- an elephant
- a baseball

KNOWLEDGE: Recall all the standard and metric units of weight you can think of; then check your list against those found in your math textbook. Add those you missed.

EVALUATION: Decide which system works best for measuring weight, the standard or the metric. Defend your position.

SYNTHESIS: Invent a new system for measuring weight. Give your units names and explain how the system works. Design a poster to advertise this new measurement system to your class.

APPLICATION: Predict in what order the following would be arranged, from the heaviest to the lightest. Then weigh each item to see if your prediction was correct.
- paper clip
- dime
- eraser
- pencil
- index card
- comb

200

Outline for an Extended Interdisciplinary Unit

Title: _____

_____

Theme: _____

_____

Objectives: _____

_____

_____

_____

Background Information for Student: _____

_____

_____

_____

_____

_____

_____

_____

Glossary: _____

_____

_____

_____

_____

_____

_____

Activities in Each Discipline (include title, objective, materials needed, procedure, and evaluation for each): _____

_____

_____

_____

(continued on next page)

Interdisciplinary Unit Outline, Page 2

_____
_____
_____
_____
_____
_____
_____
_____

Homework and/or Enrichment Ideas: _____
_____
_____
_____
_____

Directions for Post-Test or Project Presentation: _____
_____
_____
_____
_____
_____
_____

Bibliography: _____
_____
_____
_____
_____
_____
_____

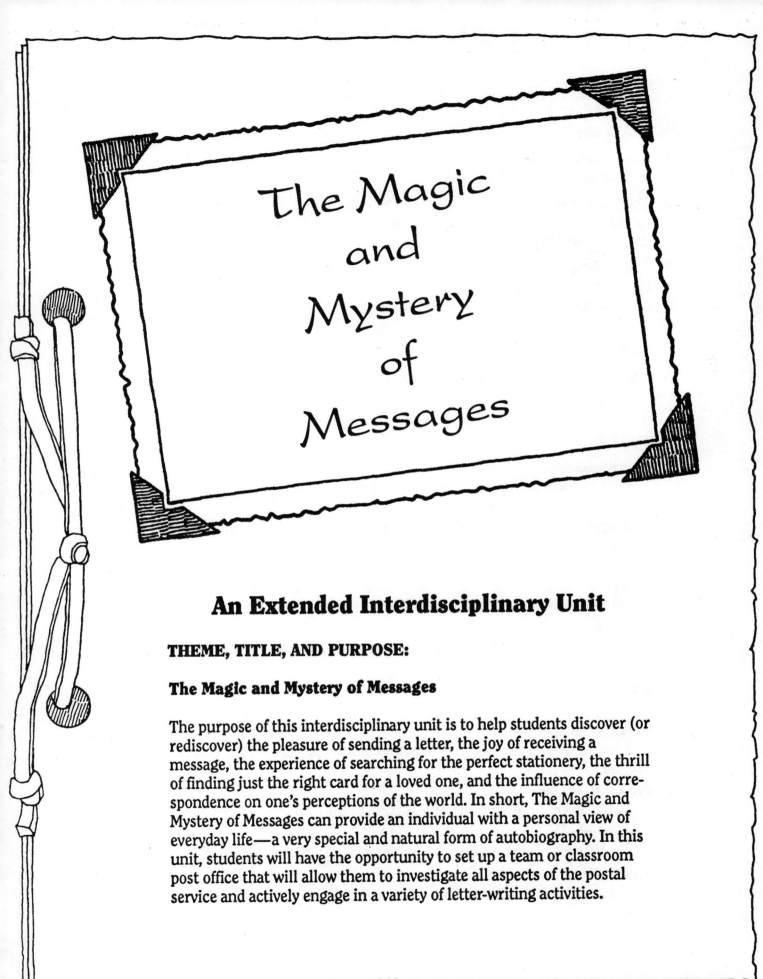

The Magic and Mystery of Messages

An Extended Interdisciplinary Unit

THEME, TITLE, AND PURPOSE:

The Magic and Mystery of Messages

The purpose of this interdisciplinary unit is to help students discover (or rediscover) the pleasure of sending a letter, the joy of receiving a message, the experience of searching for the perfect stationery, the thrill of finding just the right card for a loved one, and the influence of correspondence on one's perceptions of the world. In short, The Magic and Mystery of Messages can provide an individual with a personal view of everyday life—a very special and natural form of autobiography. In this unit, students will have the opportunity to set up a team or classroom post office that will allow them to investigate all aspects of the postal service and actively engage in a variety of letter-writing activities.

OBJECTIVES:

1. The student will examine different kinds of correspondence and practice writing according to these models.

2. The student will read selections from children's literature that are related to the "act and art of letter writing" and will use these as springboards for their own writing tasks.

3. The student will engage in a series of investigation card activities that are based on Bloom's Taxonomy and that are related to the acquisition of letter-writing skills.

4. The student will analyze the phenomenon of junk mail and its implications for the economy.

5. The student will help organize and run a classroom postal system.

GLOSSARY:

1. **Correspondence:**
   Communication through the sending and receiving of mail.

2. **Commemorative Stamp:**
   A postage stamp honoring the memory of a person, place, thing, or event.

3. **Greeting Card:**
   A card imprinted with a message and suitable illustration for use on a special holiday, celebration, or occasion.

4. **Junk Mail:**
   Third class mail such as advertisements mailed indiscriminately in large quantities.

5. **Postage:**
   The charge for mailing an item.

6. **Postage Meter:**
   A machine used to print the correct amount of postage on each piece of mail.

7. **Postal Service:**
   Mail delivery or other functions relating to the post office.

8. **Postscript:**
   A message added at the end of a letter after the writer's signature.

9. **Simulation:**
   The act or process of imitating a real-life setting or situation.

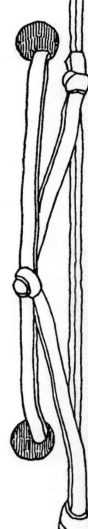

ASSESSMENT:

You will be keeping a portfolio of your work in this interdisciplinary unit. Use the Student Record-Keeping Sheet as a tool or a table of contents to help guide you in selecting artifacts for your portfolio. You must have a portfolio entry for each of the activities assigned. These entries may be first drafts, interim drafts, or final drafts of your work. You will also be expected to write a personal summary of your work expressing to the reader which items in your portfolio reflect your best efforts and which items in your portfolio reflect your less successful efforts.

STUDENT RECORD-KEEPING SHEET

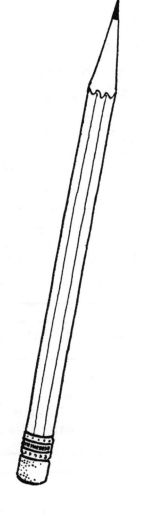

_____ ACTIVITY ONE:
      The Magic of a Letter

_____ ACTIVITY TWO:
      Practice in Letter Writing

_____ ACTIVITY THREE:
      More Practice in Letter Writing

_____ ACTIVITY FOUR:
      Designing Your Own Stationery

_____ ACTIVITY FIVE:
      Investigating a Stamp

_____ ACTIVITY SIX:
      Team Learning Activity: Junk Mail

_____ ACTIVITY SEVEN:
      Postcards as Learning Tools

_____ ACTIVITY EIGHT:
      Greeting Cards as Warm Fuzzies

_____ ACTIVITY NINE:
      Using Literature as Springboards for Letter Writing

_____ CULMINATIVE PROJECT:
      Setting Up a Classroom Post Office

_____ TAKE-HOME POST-TEST:
      My Thoughts on the Magic and Mystery of Messages

Name _____

Name _____

Activity One:
The Magic of a Letter

Take a few minutes to complete these questions individually. Then share your responses with a friend and discuss.

1. When was the last time you received a letter? sent a letter? read a letter? How did it make you feel? _____
_____
_____
_____

2. What is so special about a personal letter? How is it like and unlike a personal telephone call?_____
_____
_____
_____

3. Why don't people write more personal letters today? _____
_____
_____

4. Why is it that the busiest people seem to find the most time to communicate? _____
_____
_____

5. Can you come up with at least twenty situations in which an average person might choose to write either a friendly or a business letter to someone else?
_____
_____
_____
_____
_____
_____
_____
_____
_____
_____

Activity Two: Practice in Letter Writing

Study each of the letter-writing forms shown below. One is a business letter form and the other is a friendly letter form. Determine how they are alike and how they are different. Next, write a friendly letter to a favorite celebrity, author, or sports figure. Write a business letter requesting free or inexpensive information from the Chamber of Commerce about a place you would like to visit in the United States.

Nesbitt Creative Services
1010 Hawking Lane
Writing, Pennsylvania 24638
July 6, 1995

Eric Planter, President
National Association of Pictorial Research
P.O. Box 234
Washington, D.C. 86402

Dear Mr. Planter:

Thank you for sending me your description of services.

We are indeed interested in seeing a complete list of research categories. We are especially interested in photographs of European subjects in the first decade of the twentieth century. I will look forward to receiving the list in the mail.

Sincerely,

Barbara Robbins
Research Coordinator

BR: jp

August 28, 1995

Dear Nick,

What a great birthday gift. Thank you so much—you always seem to know exactly what I want. When you come to town, we'll play my new CD and listen to it together.

School starts in just a few days. I have a heavy load this year.

Thanks again for the CD. See you soon, I hope!

Love,

Wendy

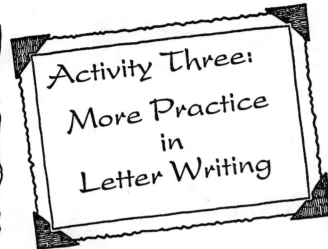

Activity Three: More Practice in Letter Writing

Today there are many variations of the traditional business and friendly letter formats. People enjoy being creative and making up their own letter-writing patterns. Choose one of the following letter-writing activities to do.

1. Write a letter to a friend, but cut pictures from magazines and paste them onto the letter to take the place of as many words as possible. Make it look like a rebus-type of correspondence.

2. Write a letter, puzzle style. After writing the letter, mount it on a file folder or piece of cardboard. On the back of the letter draw puzzle-shaped pieces. Cut them out and place them in the envelope to send.

3. Try taping a letter and sending the tape to a friend. Be sure to include anecdotes, brain teasers, jokes, riddles, and personal stories on your tape.

4. Use a secret number code to send a message to a friend. You can find number code books in the media center or you can invent a secret code of your own.

Pretend you are an artist for a greeting card company and have been asked to design a series of stationery products for students. Create a series of single-sheet designs to submit for approval to the board of directors. Create an envelope design that coordinates with each of your single-sheet designs. You can do this by reproducing the envelope pattern on page 209 and adding your own artwork for each piece.

Activity Four: Designing Your Own Stationery

Activity Five: Investigating a Stamp

Stamp collecting is both a popular hobby and an engaging career for many people throughout the world today. Postage stamp design and sales are "big business" for the postal industry on an international scale. Large quantities of cancelled stamps from every country in the world can be purchased inexpensively from stamp shops, bookstores, and hobby shops in most communities. Commemorative stamps can be purchased at cost from your local post office. To familiarize yourself with the "special world of stamps and stamp collecting," complete the set of task cards entitled "Investigating A Stamp" which are found on pages 210–213.

CUT ON THIS LINE

CUT ON THIS LINE

FOLD ON THIS LINE

FOLD ON THIS LINE

FOLD ON THIS LINE

FOLD ON THIS LINE

INVESTIGATING A STAMP

INVESTIGATING A STAMP

INVESTIGATING A STAMP

INVESTIGATING A STAMP

HOW TO USE . . .

Using a collection of various kinds of stamps, the student can choose to:

- complete only the cards which correlate to a particular level of Bloom's Taxonomy, or . . .

- select only the cards in which he or she is interested, or . . .

- (if he or she is feeling really challenged) complete all eighteen of the STAMP Investigation Cards.

Listed below are Bloom's Taxonomy Levels and the corresponding task card numbers for each.

Knowledge 1, 2, 6

Comprehension 3, 10, 16

Application.............................4, 12, 14

Analysis 8, 9, 17

Synthesis.............................7, 13, 18

Evaluation............................5, 11, 15

210

1

Select any five stamps
from the collection.

Write a detailed description
of each stamp.

Put each description
on a file card.

Have a friend match each stamp
with each description.

2

Take the collection of stamps and
rearrange them into small groups.
The stamps in each small group
must have something in common
with the other stamps
in that same group.

Make a list of the groups you have,
the members in each group,
and the criteria or common
characteristics that account for
each group.

3

Suggest reasons
that explain why a person
might develop a passion for
stamp collecting.

4

Select any five stamps
from your stamp collection.

Ask ten people to choose
their favorite stamps
from the five
you have selected.

Graph the results of your
"favorite stamp" survey.

5

What do you think it means to put
one's "stamp of approval" on things?

Where and how do you think the
above expression originated?

Name five things in your classroom
or your school on which you would
put your "stamp of approval."

Be ready to defend
each of your choices.

6

Outline the steps you would take
to begin and maintain
a high-quality stamp collection.

7

Select any five stamps
from the collection.

Arrange the stamps in any order
you wish and then create
a cartoon or comic strip
using the stamps as illustrations
or key checkpoints.

8

Select any five stamps
from the collection and write ten
subtle words to describe each stamp.

Put each set of ten words
on a separate file card
or piece of paper.

Ask a friend to inspect or examine
each stamp and each list of words.

Can he or she deduce
which stamp goes with
each set of descriptive words?

9

Study the stamps
in your collection.
Write the criteria you think are
used by the U.S. Postal Service
to determine which people,
places, objects, or events
become subject matter for
stamp designs.

10

Define the word or concept
"stamp"
in your own words.

11

Select any ten stamps from the
collection and rank order them from
the most important stamp to the
least important stamp. Be able to give
3 to 5 reasons for your first choice or
most important stamp and your
last choice or least important stamp.

Next, give your ten stamps
to a friend and have him or her
do the same thing.

Do you agree on the rank ordering?
Do you agree on the first and last
choice selection? Why or why not?

12

Predict how many stamps
from your collection
it would take to cover
the surface of one of your
school books.

Test your prediction.

13

Most stamps are indeed
works of art.
Design an original stamp
celebrating
a famous person, place,
thing, or event.

14

Commemorative postage stamps
are colorful and decorative. An easy
way to dress up an envelope is to use
the picture on the postage stamp as
the idea for your envelope decoration.
If the stamp pictures a fish you might
draw a fish swimming around the
address. Pick a stamp with a picture
that looks like part of a larger scene
and draw the rest of the scene on the
envelope. Color the scene to match
the colors that are on the stamp.
Choose a stamp from your collection
and apply one of these techniques to
demonstrate your understanding of
the stamp's content.

15

Select one stamp from the
collection that best represents
each of the following ideas:

a. a symbol of leadership

b. a symbol of beauty

c. a symbol of hope or peace

d. a symbol of fame or fortune

e. a symbol of nature

f. justice

16

List the subject matter
depicted on each of the stamps
in your collection.

Put your list
in alphabetical order.

17

Analyze your feelings by relating
these "Stamp of Approval" statements
to you and your friends.

1. I'd like to stamp out . . . because . . .

2. I put my stamp of approval on . . .
because . . .

3. I don't give a lick about . . .
because . . .

4. I'm stuck on . . .

5. I'd like to get a special delivery
of . . . ; then I could . . .

6. _____ and I stick together when . . .

7. _____ is first class with me!

18

Haiku is a Japanese form of poetry
that has three short lines or phrases.
The first line has five syllables,
the second line has seven syllables,
and the third line has five syllables.

Choose a stamp and use it
as a springboard for writing
an original haiku.

Activity Six:
Team Learning Activity:
Junk Mail

You are to work with your cooperative learning group of three members to examine a Letter to the Editor from a reader who feels that junk mail is a costly nuisance. To complete this activity, follow these steps:

Step 1: Appoint a Reader, Recorder, and Timekeeper in your group so that each group member has a job.

Step 2: The Recorder uses the Recording Sheet "Junk Mail" to write down the responses of your group's best thinking. Be sure to write the names of both the Recorder and the Team Members in the spaces provided for this purpose.

Step 3: The Reader takes the responsibility for guiding the group through the reading of the Letter to the Editor and making certain that all group members understand its message.

Step 4: The Timekeeper makes certain that all group members stay on task and complete their discussion and responses to the four questions in a timely fashion.

Step 5: When all questions have been completed and written on the Recording Sheet, all group members sign their names on the sheet to indicate they all contributed to the task and agree with the written responses.

TEAM LEARNING ACTIVITY: JUNK MAIL

OBJECTIVE

To examine a Letter to the Editor from a reader who feels junk mail is a costly nuisance.

TEAM MEMBERS

1. _____

2. _____

3. _____

Recorder_____

ASSIGNMENT

Read the Letter to the Editor below from M. R. Turner of North Port. Use it to answer (as a group) the questions on page 216.

NEWS LOCAL NEWS — LETTERS

PAGE 10

JANUARY 14

Unsolicited 'Junk' Mail Is a Costly Nuisance

During the month of February we received 74 pieces of mail, all unsolicited, sent at rates ranging from approximately five cents to 10 to 15 cents. The 29-cent stamps we use on our mail obviously helps subsidize this "junk" mail.

Of the 74 pieces referred to above, 58 were nonpolitical, all asking for money. Many of the requests were from well-known charities, and we contribute modestly to a number of these. But, I keep hearing from groups I didn't know existed!

The selling of mailing lists is big business, and once you support some of these causes, you're on these lists. How do you get your name removed?

During February, two groups sent us three appeals, and eight sent out two mailings! It makes you wonder what percentage of every dollar collected goes for overhead. I suspect it's greatly over 50 percent in too many instances.

By and large, Americans are very generous, but it seems this trait is being greatly exploited by greedy operators. How does one know which appeals are legitimate?

All this "junk" mail certainly places an added burden on our postal system, which ultimately will mean higher postal rates for you and me. Why not charge this flood of unsolicited mail rates such as you and I pay? It would greatly reduce the quantity of such mail, and would eliminate the inefficient and borderline operators.

M. R. TURNER
North Port

1. What is the major purpose of M. R. Turner's letter?

_____

_____

_____

_____

_____

2. What evidence does M. R. Turner give to support his or her viewpoint?

_____

_____

_____

_____

_____

3. Do you agree with M. R. Turner's position? Why or why not?

_____

_____

_____

_____

_____

_____

4. If your group were to set guidelines for the type of junk mail which could be sent at reduced rates, what would they be? List at least 3 to 5 recommendations.

1. _____

2. _____

3. _____

4. _____

5. _____

We all agree with the responses to the above questions.

Signature of Team Member 1 _____

Signature of Team Member 2 _____

Signature of Team Member 3 _____

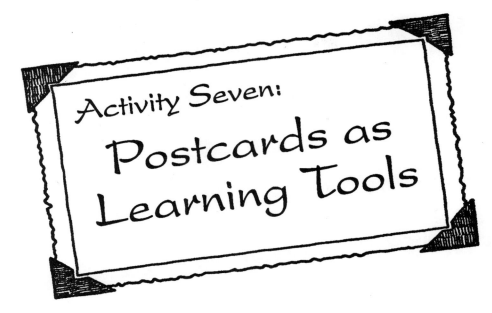

Activity Seven:
Postcards as Learning Tools

Did you know that postcards come in several different flavors or types just as ice cream does at an ice cream shop? One can find "scratch and sniff" postcards, travel postcards, greeting postcards, joke postcards, art postcards, and even do-it-yourself postcards. In this activity, you will explore some of the great art masterpieces of the world by using an assortment of postcards depicting famous artists and their works. These postcard collections can be purchased in most bookstores and art museums in any community. Use your postcard collection to complete each of the tasks listed below. Write your responses on a separate piece of paper.

1. Select a postcard picture that you think would look best in our classroom. Write a paragraph justifying your choice.

2. Select a postcard picture and compile a list of words to vividly describe its content. Mix up the postcards in your collection and ask a friend to try to match your word list with the picture it depicts.

3. Select a postcard picture that either makes you feel cheerful, sad, confused, or lonely. Explain how the artist used color, line, perspective, light, and subject matter to create this mood.

4. Select a postcard picture that seems to tell a story. Write a short essay explaining what that story is about. Include events that might have happened both before and after the scene in the painting.

5. Select two postcard pictures that appear to be on the same topic, theme, setting, or genre. Compare and contrast the two different works.

6. Select a postcard picture and write a series of math word problems based on a person, place, or thing in the painting.

Now . . . use the blank postcard patterns on the following pages to create an original piece of modern art. Try to make it reflect a particular content area such as math, science, social studies, home economics, or language arts. For example, you might use geometric shapes for math, alphabet letters for language arts, plant life for science, kitchen utensils for home economics, or cultural symbols for social studies as the basic visual stimulus. Draw your picture on the front of the postcard (page 218) and explain it on the postcard's back (page 219).

STAMP

To:

Activity Eight: Greeting Cards as Warm Fuzzies

Greeting cards are a wonderful form of correspondence and come in a variety of colors, shapes, sizes, and formats. Today people send greeting cards to celebrate everything from birthdays and graduations to retirements and foreign travel experiences. Use a collection of five to ten greeting cards to complete each of the following tasks. Record your responses on a separate piece of paper.

1. **Knowledge Level Task:**
   Visit a store that sells greeting cards and make a list of all the different types of greeting cards that you see on the shelves.

2. **Comprehension Level Task:**
   Compare and contrast the illustrations and messages of at least two greeting cards in your collection.

3. **Application Level Task:**
   Compute the total cost, including tax, of the greeting cards in your collection.

4. **Analysis Level Task:**
   Analyze the placement of the messages on the greeting cards in your collection. How do they differ and why?

5. **Synthesis Level Task:**
   Make up a new and special occasion for which a greeting card could be sent. Name your occasion, tell how you would promote it, and design an original greeting to send.

6. **Evaluation Level Task:**
   Rank the following types of correspondence from your favorite to receive (which is one) to your least favorite to receive (which is five). Explain your choices.

   _____ a. Letter
   _____ b. Invitation
   _____ c. Personal note
   _____ d. Postcard
   _____ e. Greeting card

Activity Nine:

Using Literature as Springboards for Letter Writing

Many books for both children and adults have been written about the "magic and mystery of receiving a message." Three of these literary works are included on the following pages. Read each of these special books and write your reactions to each one in the space provided below. Then select one of the three book options to complete in more detail. Be prepared to answer all QUESTIONS and finish all ACTIVITIES required on the assignment sheet.

1. My reactions to the book *Where's Waldo?* by Martin Handford.

_____
_____
_____
_____
_____

2. My reactions to the book *The Jolly Postman or Other People's Letters* by Janet & Allen Ahlberg.

_____
_____
_____
_____
_____

3. My reactions to the book *P.S. I Love You* compiled by H. Jackson Brown, Jr.

_____
_____
_____
_____

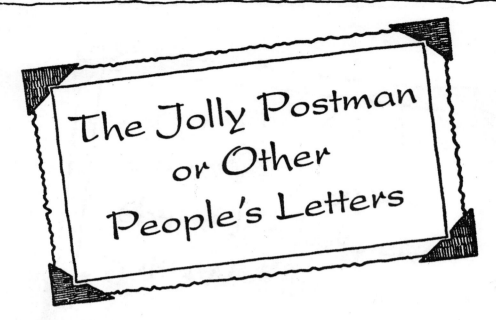

The Jolly Postman or Other People's Letters

SOURCE

The Jolly Postman or Other People's Letters by Janet and Allen Ahlberg. Boston, MA: Little, Brown and Company, 1986.

SYNOPSIS

The Jolly Postman has delivered the mail. What could possibly be in the letter from Goldilocks to the Three Bears? There is a message for the Wicked Witch, but who would write to her? When reading this book, take out the letters, each from its envelope, and you'll discover which well-known fairy tale characters have written to each other.

QUESTIONS

1. What is most unusual about this book?
2. Which letter was your favorite and why?
3. What clues do you have that this book was written and published first in London before it was published in the United States?
4. Which of the fairy tale characters was most familiar to you?
5. How have fairy tales enriched our culture, childhood, or imaginations?
6. When you were a child, what was your favorite fairy tale and why?

ACTIVITIES

1. Choose any two of the following fairy tales to read or review. Then write a letter, Janet and Allen Ahlberg-style, from one main character to another. Be creative with the letter format you use, the message you send, the stationery you use, the address you put on the envelope, and the stamp/postmark you design.

Snow White	*Jack and the Beanstalk*	*Sleeping Beauty*
The Little Mermaid	*The Little Red Hen*	*Cinderella*
Puss 'n' Boots	*The Three Little Pigs*	*The Gingerbread Man*
The Ugly Duckling	*Little Red Riding Hood*	*Bluebeard*
The Shoemaker and the Elves	*Goldilocks and the*	*Tom Thumb*
Rapunzel	*Three Bears*	*Dick Whittington*
Hansel and Gretel	*The Three Billy Goats Gruff*	*The Frog Prince*

2. Work with a group of friends and combine your letters into a book similar to *The Jolly Postman*. How will you tie everything together?
3. Try writing a Jolly Postman book with letters between historical figures writing about historical events, or mythological characters writing about myths, or scientists writing about important medical discoveries.

Where's Waldo?

SOURCE

Where's Waldo? by Martin Handford. Boston, MA: Little, Brown, and Co., 1987

SYNOPSIS

The reader follows Waldo as he hikes around the world and must try to find him in the illustrations of the crowded places he visits. Each destination is introduced with a letter to the reader by Waldo himself.

QUESTIONS

1. Who is Waldo? How would you describe his appearance and personality?
2. What places does he visit in this book?
3. What role do the letters from Waldo play in the overall theme of the book?
4. Why is it difficult to find Waldo in each setting? Which was the most difficult for you? the easiest for you?
5. What are some other places you can think of for Waldo to visit in the next edition of this book?

ACTIVITIES

1. Work with a friend to create another page for the book *Where's Waldo?* Don't forget to include a letter along with the graphics.
2. Try creating your own version of *Where's Waldo?* by inventing an original character from another country/culture, another period in history, or another setting such as outer space. Try writing a set of clues with descriptive language and specific directions for finding the character as part of each letter.

SOURCE

P.S. I Love You (When Mom Wrote She Always Saved the Best for Last). Compiled by H. Jackson Brown, Jr., Nashville, TN: Rutledge Hill Press, 1990.

SYNOPSIS

This book comes from a collection of letters written by a mother to her daughters. It contains only the P.S. (postscript) notes that she wrote at the end of each letter. There, in just a few words, she encourages and inspires the girls with her keen observations, gentle humor, and loving advice.

QUESTIONS

1. What kind of person do you think the mother was? Why do you think so?
2. In what ways do you think the daughters benefited from their mother's "words of wisdom"?
3. Have you ever saved letters from a sender? If so, why?
4. Which of the postscripts is your favorite? Give reasons for your choice.
5. What are some of the values which the mother passes on to her daughters through the postscripts?

ACTIVITIES

1. Organize a post office for your classroom whereby you and your friends can send notes and letters to one another on a regular basis. Try to include a P.S. for each message you send. What will you use for a mailbox and what corner of the room will serve as the post office? Who will work in the post office as the mailman, the seller of stamps, the sorter, and the canceller of mail?
2. Create your own version of *P.S. I Love You* with a series of postscripts to a family member, a relative, a friend, or a favorite adult. Include examples of your favorite bumper sticker sayings, quotations, proverbs, poems, greeting card sayings, jokes, signs, advertisements, and personal experiences.
3. Try writing a *P.S. I Love You* with a different twist. Consider a book from the President to the citizens of the United States. Consider a book from Snoopy to Charlie Brown. Consider a book from George Washington to Abraham Lincoln. Consider a book from a student to a teacher. Consider a book from a major league baseball player to a little league player. Consider a book from a Martian to an Earth person.

SETTING UP A CLASSROOM POST OFFICE

As a culminating activity for this unit, you and your classmates will set up a working post office for your school or classroom. To help you get started, work with a small or large group of peers and outline the steps needed to complete this task. The questions listed will need to be addressed as part of your planning process.

1. Where will the post office be housed and what hours will it keep?

2. What different jobs will be needed to operate the post office and who will handle these responsibilities?

3. What physical set-up or facility will be needed and what equipment and tools will be required to make it function?

4. What types of services will your post office provide the customer? Consider mail delivery, post office boxes, sale of stamps, distribution of packages, and money orders.

5. What kinds of mail will be distributed by the post office and what rules or guidelines will be established for monitoring this process?

6. How will the post office venture be financed?

7. When will the post office officially open and how long will it be in existence?

TAKE-HOME POST-TEST

My Thoughts on
the Magic and Mystery of Messages

Directions To Student: You are to complete this post-test by using time at home and at school. You will have two days to do your work.

PART I

1. The main differences between a business letter and a friendly letter are _____

_____

_____

_____

_____

2. The advantages of communicating by letter or mail versus communicating by telephone are _____

_____

_____

_____

3. Correspondence can be personalized in many ways by doing things such as __

_____

_____

_____

4. The only time I ever write letters or send messages is _____

_____

_____

_____

5. I would like to receive a letter from _____

telling me _____

_____

_____

_____

_____

_____

6. The seven "Cs" of good letters are clear, correct, complete, courteous, concise, conversational, and considerate. Can you think of seven or more other descriptive words relating to letter writing that do not begin with "C"? What are they? _____

_____

_____

_____

_____

PART II

Write both a business letter and a friendly letter by choosing from the options listed below.

LANGUAGE ARTS

A friendly letter to an author of your favorite book telling what you like best about his or her books and style of writing.

MATH

A friendly letter to an adult you know who used math in his or her work asking him or her to personally tell you why math is a key in job success.

SOCIAL STUDIES

A business letter to a government official in your community stating an opinion on a political issue of special interest to young people.

SCIENCE

A business letter to a local library, museum, or science facility asking for information about its student offerings and programs.

Name _____

Themes for Interdisciplinary Units

SCIENCE

Volcanoes
Hurricanes
Floods
Wind
Weather
Natural Disasters
Smart Food, Junk Food
Oceanography
Robotics
Rain Forests
Conservation
Prehistoric Plants
Space Exploration
Energy
Nature's Follies
Mountain Majesty
The Desert's Secrets
Animals on the Move
Communication in Nature
Kitchen Chemistry
How's the Weather?
What's a Body To Do?
Power Plug
What Goes Up Must Come Down

SOCIAL STUDIES

The Egyptian Heritage
Awesome Africa
The Grandeur of Greece
Ancient Civilizations
China, Then and Now
Industrialization
People of the Past
Famous World Heroes
Famous Women
Futurism
Transportation
Consumerism
Rights and Responsibilities
Worldwide Adventures
Monumental Places
Circling the Globe
Kids at Work
Order in the Court
Know Your Rights
People at a Glance
People—Rank and File
The Generation Gap

LANGUAGE ARTS

Communication Countdown
Conflict Resolution
Secret Languages/Mystery
    Messages
Greetings Around the World
Magazine Madness
Television: Turn On or Turn Off?
The Record Racket
Folklore
Storytelling and Storytellers
Language of the Environment
Legacies and Legends
Fact or Fiction
Write Your Way Out
Poetry Pack Rat
A Body Speaks Louder Than Words
Autographs and Biographs
Reader's Choice
Library Lingo
Nose for the News
Catalog Capers
Dictionary Dig

EXPLORATORY

Great Museums of the World
Computer Technology
Sports
Travel
Fads and Fashions
Ethnic Food
Codes and Ciphers
Endangered Species
Superstitions
Say What You Mean
    (Colorful Language)
What's In a Name?
Traditions and Celebrations
The Martial Arts
Places of Pain and Pleasure
Disasters and Diseases
Earth Recipes and Natural Recipes
Knights in Shining Armor
Colors of the World
Decorator Dilemmas

MATH

As Time Goes By
Symmetry
Optical Illusions
Geometry in Nature and the
    Environment
Number Play
Tessellations
Weighty Matters
Problem-Solving
Money Matters
How Much Did Peter Piper Pick?
What's Missing?

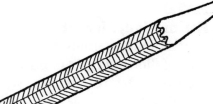

Ideas for Using Yellow Pages To Teach or Reinforce Content Area Skills and/or Concepts

1. ALL SUBJECTS:

Brainstorming

Make a list of twelve situations in which you might use the telephone Yellow Pages to save time and/or money. Beside each situation, list the information you would need from the Yellow Pages.

2. MATH:

Estimation, Measurement

Estimate the amount of Yellow Page space (area on a page) devoted to each of the following types of businesses and check to see if your estimates are correct. Before you make your estimate, measure the square inches on a typical Yellow Page.

- Toys
- Laundries
- Dentists
- Hairdressers
- Men's clothing

3. ALL SUBJECTS:
Research

Use the Yellow Pages to plan a perfect Saturday for you and a best friend. Plan where you will go, what you will do, what you will eat, and what you will see. Then use your Yellow Pages again to confirm addresses, times, prices, and other needed information.

4. SOCIAL STUDIES:
Recognizing Individual Differences

Create a Yellow Pages directory for students in your class. Have each student design a display ad promoting some skill, talent, expertise, hobby, or interest he or she would be willing to share with others.

5. SOCIAL STUDIES:
Decision Making, Rating

Appraise the usefulness of the Yellow Pages. Design a scale to rate its usefulness to students of your age, younger children, parents, teachers, tourists from out of town, advertisers, and government agencies.

6. SCIENCE:
Environmental Awareness

Create a Green Pages directory for your community offering sales, services, and information related to environmental awareness. Be thorough and creative in designing the lists and ads to encourage people to be better consumers and more careful conservationists.

7. LANGUAGE ARTS:
Critical Reading

Critique and criticize the Yellow Pages in your phone directory and make a list of recommendations for improving its usefulness and overall appeal. Pretend you have been hired as a consultant to upgrade the revision and that your recommendations are to be followed just as you present them. Include cover suggestions complete with color, type, size, and style; information and illustration; size and shape; organization; types of ads and amount of space to be allocated to ads; and information of interest to the user such as zip codes, holidays, etc.

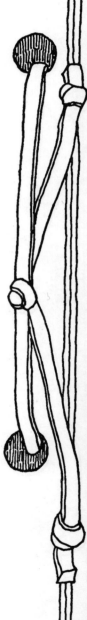

8. LANGUAGE ARTS:

Reading for Specific Information, Summarizing, Creative Writing

Find out about your community's eating habits and interests by consulting the Yellow Pages. Count and list the expensive restaurants, fast food restaurants, health food restaurants, pizza parlors, and ethnic restaurants. Find out which there are more of, which ones spend the most money on advertising, and where the most restaurants of one type are located. For example, use a map to find out in what part of town most of the expensive restaurants are located, where you would be most apt to find an Italian or Mexican restaurant, and where you would go for the best pizza. Write a paragraph summarizing your findings and stating your opinion of the food interests of the residents of your town.

9. WRITING:

Descriptive Writing

Design a creative Yellow Pages ad for one of the following businesses. Limit the message to sixty-five words and use the most descriptive and compelling words possible.
- Electric Repair Shop
- Tuxedo Rental Service
- Carpet Cleaner
- Skateboard Shop
- Snow Removal Service
- Landscape Designer

10. MATH:

Estimation, Figuring Areas

Quickly scan the Yellow Pages in your directory that are composed of advertising. Look at the size of the ads and count the number of pages. Estimate how many businesses are advertised and write down your estimate. Then count the ads to see how close you were. It sounds tedious but can actually be a lot of fun. Besides, think of how impressed your friends will be when you pass on this piece of trivia . . . "Did you know our Yellow Pages include _____ paid advertisements?"

Ideas for Using the Newspaper To Teach or Reinforce Content Area Skills and Concepts

1. READING:
Identifying Character Traits

Use the Sunday comic section to find character traits:

... a character who is friendly, outgoing, and obliging

... a dialogue showing a person with a sense of humor and/or exhibiting a positive outlook on life

... a character you would consider trustworthy

... a character you would identify as unrealistic or out of touch with the group

Choose your favorite character and your least favorite character and explain why you feel as you do.

2. READING:
Comprehension

Turn to the obituary section and scan the page. Select three obituaries that interest you the most. Note the facts presented and the language usage in each. Is there a pattern in the way in which the facts are presented? Find the birthplaces, ages, and occupations of each if you can. Compare and contrast these facts. Try to visualize the basic style of each person.

ing

...ter from the "Letters to the Editor" page that interests you. Read it carefully, and then write two letters: one to the Editor of the newspaper that you would be willing to have published and one to the author of the letter. In each letter, state your response to the letter writer's position on the topic of the letter. Remember, think the issue through and be sure your opinion is a responsible one that you could justify and defend.

4. LANGUAGE ARTS:
Critical Reading/Creative Writing

Study the front page of your local newspaper. Plan and lay out the front page of a newspaper for your classroom using *today's* news as your content. To be sure you include all the pertinent information for a front page, make a checklist before you begin, including title, date, headlines, list of contents, etc. Write your articles carefully to reflect news of importance to the intended readers: your teachers and classmates.

5. THINKING:
Decision Making

Read the entire newspaper carefully. Decide:
... which section is of the most interest to kids of your age.
... which section is most important for all adults to read on a daily basis.
... who reads the comics.
... how much difference it would make to the average reader if the newspaper was not published for a month.

After you have made your decisions, write one brief paragraph stating the criteria used in your decision-making and defend your decisions in keeping with the criteria.

6. SOCIAL STUDIES:
Critiquing Current Events

Draw a cartoon to state a concern you have about a social issue of importance to students of your age.

7. SCIENCE:
Weather Forecasting

Study the weather forecast for the next three days. Note and record the actual temperatures and conditions and compare with the predictions to determine their accuracy.

How would the discrepancies affect farmers, fishermen, baseball players, construction workers, and/or you?

8. MATH:
Problem-Solving/Money

Use the classified ad section of yesterday's newspaper to do a little comparative shopping. Compare the cost of used cars with the cost of new ones. Compare like makes of automobiles and find out how much difference a year's wear and tear makes and how much difference ten years makes and try to determine the best buys in terms of years, makes, and models. For example, would it be more profitable to buy the same make and year model station wagon, pickup truck, convertible, or sedan?

Then, just for fun, select the car from all those advertised that you would most like to own and try to figure out how much it would cost you to maintain it for one year if by some miracle you could purchase it today. Don't forget to include license, insurance, gasoline, and maintenance in the cost.

9. READING:
Scanning, Reading for a Specific Purpose

Scan an entire newspaper. Give examples of one specific article or section that is used to do each of the following: inform, entertain, persuade, educate the reader.

10. SOCIAL STUDIES:
Self Awareness

Construct a mini-newspaper all about yourself that includes a news story, a feature story, a comic strip, a cartoon, an editorial, a classified section. Remember, this is your newspaper.

11. ALL SUBJECTS:
Creating, Composing

Make a learning poster that includes a sample news story, feature story, editorial, cartoon, display ad, classified ad, stock market report, book review, restaurant review, weather forecast, and index. Label each section appropriately.

12. WRITING:
Newspaper Article

Write a newspaper article for your school's newspaper using one of the following topics:
... How kids really feel about math (as taught in your school) and its relevance to the real world
... The fairness of your school's rules and their effect on student behavior
... The effectiveness of worldwide conservation efforts and ways the average citizen could contribute to saving our natural resources
... The effect of junk food on the health and welfare of citizens today

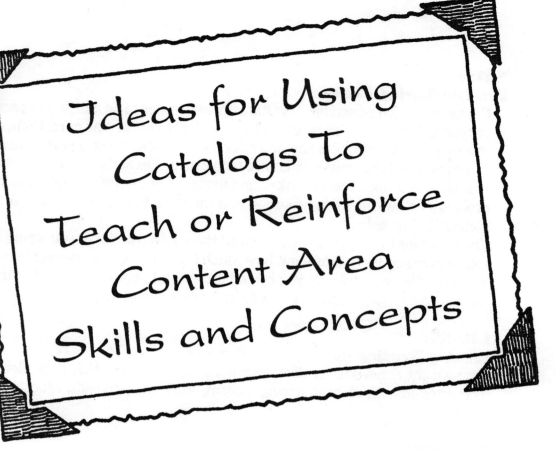

Ideas for Using Catalogs To Teach or Reinforce Content Area Skills and Concepts

1. **LANGUAGE ARTS:**
   Reading, Writing, Visualizing, Drawing

   Select one catalog to look through carefully. Note the types, prices, and diversity of the merchandise offered. Then write a description of a person you think would be likely to shop from this particular catalog. Draw a picture of the person using one item from the catalog.

2. **MATH:**
   Problem-Solving, Addition

   Select a catalog of interest to people of your age. Pretend that you have been given $350 to spend on surprise gifts for six friends. List each friend's name and then select (from the catalog) a gift for each. Remember, you have only $350 to spend, so you will have to shop carefully to make your money come out evenly, including shipping and handling charges for each purchase. Oh, yes, the one stipulation is that you must spend the entire sum of $350—you must have less than $2.57 left over.

3. SOCIAL STUDIES:
Consumerism, Comparison Shopping

Look through three or four catalogs of interest to you. Make a list of ten items you would like to order. Then list the reasons you would buy these items directly from catalogs rather than from stores in your community. On a separate sheet of paper, list reasons for shopping for the items in the retail outlets in your community. Compare the two lists and weigh the advantages of each to decide if you are a prospective catalog shopper.

After your decision is made, go over the list of items again, weighing each carefully to see if it would be a wise purchase. Divide the items into two categories, want and need. Are you a wise buyer? If not, what steps could you take to become a responsible buyer?

4. SCIENCE:
Conservation, Evaluation

Select a catalog featuring articles for sports-minded nature lovers and/or camping equipment buyers. Go through the catalog to determine which of the items would harm the natural environment, which could be recycled, and which would conserve the Earth's natural resources. Develop criteria for evaluating the catalog's influence on our planet Earth and give the catalog an overall rating.

5. SOCIAL STUDIES/ART:
Responsible Consumerism Art

Design a catalog cover to attract socially aware buyers of household and garden products that are safe for the environment and designed to make the best use of the Earth's natural resources. Name your catalog and state its mission on the front cover.

6. SOCIAL STUDIES/WRITING:
Futurism

Some people predict that electronic shopping by television will replace mail-order catalogs within the next twenty to thirty years. Write a brief essay giving your opinion of this prediction. Consider changing lifestyles and changing needs for consumer items when forming your opinions.

7. THINKING:
Decision Making

Examine at least five catalogs from cover to cover to determine the six most important factors in producing an effective catalog. Remember, the effective catalog is the one that makes the reader feel he or she just has to place an order. Make a list of all the factors you consider important and select the top six from that list.

8. ALL SUBJECTS:
Research
> Try to find answers for these questions:
> ... What effect does the mass mailing of catalogs have on conservation of natural resources?
> ... What happens to undeliverable catalogs mailed through the U.S. Postal System?
> ... How do catalog companies secure addresses of potential buyers?

9. ALL SUBJECTS:
Visualizing, Designing
> Catalogs are becoming more specialized every year. Design a catalog cover and a sample page for one of these specialty markets:
> ... computer game buffs
> ... mystery lovers
> ... number maniacs or problem-solvers
> ... armchair travelers
> ... would-be best dressers

10. CREATIVE WRITING:
Story Writing
> Use one of the following story starters to write the most imaginative mystery story you can. (Don't forget Who, When, Where, Why, and How.)
>> It all happened because the great catalog monster ...
>>
>> I found this strange catalog beside ...
>>
>> I never expected my order to arrive by ...
>>
>> I dreamed that I was surrounded up to my neck by catalogs and ...
>>
>> I was surprised to find my picture on that catalog cover ...

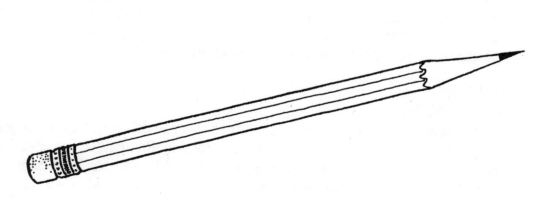

Ideas for Using Magazine Ads To Teach or Reinforce Content Area Skills and Concepts

1. LANGUAGE ARTS:
Reading and Writing

Browse through a set of magazines from your home, school, or community library to see the different types of ads that appear on their pages. Take notes as you do your browsing by completing each of the starter statements below:

    a. Magazine ads that get my attention are those that . . .
    b. Advertising in magazines is most helpful to me when . . .
    c. Products that seem to appear in a majority of the magazine ads I saw were . . .
    d. My favorite magazine ad of those that I saw was . . . because . .
    e. I wish magazine advertisers would . . .

2. SOCIAL STUDIES:
Propaganda Techniques

Browse through a set of magazines from your home, school, or community library and find a sample ad for each of the propaganda techniques listed below. Cut these out and paste each one onto a separate piece of plain notebook or drawing paper. Label each ad with its appropriate propaganda technique. Keep this "mini-scrapbook" of ads for use with the following activities.

PROPAGANDA ON PARADE

- **Analogy**—This used car has 30,000 miles on it, so it will be better than the one with 55,000 miles.

- **Bandwagon**—Don't miss this sale; EVERYONE will be there!

- **Ego Trip**—It costs more, but you're worth it!
- **Emotional Appeal**—There have been reports of burglaries in town—call BUR–GLAR for your burglar alarm today.
- **Exaggeration**—Don't miss the sale of a lifetime; come in today.
- **Generalizations**—EVERYONE is hurrying to ABC Department store to get in on the sale.
- **Half Truths Clearance**—Everything 50% off. (What the ad doesn't tell you is that "everything" refers to last season's styles.)
- **Name Dropping**—Mr. X (a famous quarterback) uses this product.
- **Repetition**—Using slogans again and again.
- **Snob Appeal**—For those who want the very best!
- **Testimonials**—Recommended by 3 out of 4 doctors.
- **Vagueness**—Everyone is talking about our new model. (But what are they saying?)

3. SOCIAL STUDIES:
Drawing Conclusions

Examine your "mini-scrapbook" of ads and draw a set of conclusions concerning why each advertiser chose the technique that he or she used in each advertisement. Make an inference as to who you think was the intended audience. Write your conclusions on a separate piece of paper and include it as an additional page in your "mini-scrapbook."

4. MATHEMATICS:
Money

Magazine advertising space is expensive to buy. Generally speaking, a full page ad in color costs about $8000.00 and in black & white costs about $5000.00. A ½ page ad in color costs about $4500.00 and in black & white costs about $3000.00. A ⅓ page ad in color costs about $2500.00 and in black & white costs about $1800.00. Using these figures as a guide, determine the total cost of your entire "mini-scrapbook" of ads. Write your findings in an interesting way and include this as an additional page in your "mini-scrapbook."

5. LANGUAGE ARTS AND SOCIAL STUDIES:
Creative Writing

Select one of the ads from your "mini-scrapbook" and develop totally new copy for this ad using a propaganda technique different from the one used by the advertiser. Write your new ad copy and paste it on the page next to the original one in the "mini-scrapbook."

6. SCIENCE:
Fact vs. Opinion

Examine each of the ads from your "mini-scrapbook" and underline those parts of each ad that seem to express either a scientific fact or a scientific opinion about

the product. If any of the ads do not include a science-related fact or opinion, try writing one that might fit in each instance. Add these original science-related facts and opinions to the bottom of each ad in the "mini-scrapbook."

7. LANGUAGE ARTS:
Figurative Language
Study your "mini-scrapbook" of ads, looking for examples of figurative language in each of them. Advertisers often use similes, metaphors, alliteration, personification, and analogies in their copy. Write these down on a separate piece of paper and include as an additional page in your "mini-scrapbook."

8. LANGUAGE ARTS:
Writing Quotations
Imagine what a magazine ad might say to a television commercial, a classified ad in the newspaper, a highway billboard, and a neon sign. Write a conversation among these varied forms of advertising media, using the appropriate quotation marks and punctuation.

9. ALL SUBJECT AREAS:
Evaluation
Rank order each of the magazine ads in your "mini-scrapbook" from one to ten with one being the best ad and ten being the worst ad. In making your decisions, be sure to consider each of the following criteria for ad design: effective use of color, figurative language, facts, testimonials, customer needs/satisfaction, value, cost, and authenticity. Write your evaluation in a chart, graph, or report format, giving reasons for your first and last choices.

10. ALL SUBJECT AREAS:
Designing a Magazine Ad
Pretend you have just been given the opportunity to design an ad for students your age that will be used by one of the largest public relation firms in the community. If your ad is successful, you will be given a gift certificate of $1000.00 to a local retail store of your choice. Select one of the following options for your ad and make it special. What propaganda technique will you use and how will you make the ad a high-quality one?

LANGUAGE ARTS: Create a magazine ad to promote more reading and less television viewing in the home.

SOCIAL STUDIES: Create a magazine ad to advocate paying students a minimum wage for attending school and doing their work.

MATHEMATICS: Create a magazine ad to show students the importance of math in their daily lives.

 SCIENCE: Create a magazine ad to discourage littering of public places most frequented by young people.

Ideas for Using
Menus To
Teach or Reinforce
Content Area
Skills and Concepts

You will need a collection of at least five menus for completing this set of activities.

1. LANGUAGE ARTS:
Reading/Writing/Drawing Conclusions
Read the menus in your collection and use them as a source of information to complete each of the following starter statements:
   a. An attractive or appealing menu is one that . . .
   b. A nutritious menu must have . . .
   c. A menu can be a sales or marketing tool for a restaurant if it . . .
   d. The menu I would most enjoy selecting a meal from is . . because . . .
   e. These menus could be improved if they would only . . .

2. ART:
Designing an Ad
Create an unusual newspaper or magazine ad to promote one of the restaurants in your collection of menus. Make it colorful, dramatic, and eye-catching.

3. MATH:
Computation of Whole Numbers
Select one of the menus and order a meal for each member of your family from it based on what you know about their food preferences and eating habits. Compute the number of calories that would be consumed in each meal, using a calorie counter or calorie chart.

4. SCIENCE:
Comparison and Contrast
Compare and contrast any two of the menus in your collection by examining the nutritional value of the foods available. Consider such nutritional elements as: food groups, calories, fat grams, nutrients, taste, light/heavy fare, and dietary needs.

5. MATH:
Charts and Graphs
Survey ten members of your class to find out which of the five menus has the most appeal to them and why. Chart or graph your findings in some way.

6. MATH:
Money
Plan a birthday party for yourself and five friends at one of the restaurants represented in your collection of menus. Choose a complete meal to be served to all six of you. Determine the cost of each meal. Determine the total amount of the bill, including sales tax (for your state) and the amount of the tip (at fifteen percent).

7. SOCIAL STUDIES:
Occupations
Choose one of the menus from the collection and think about all of the different jobs or occupations that were involved in making this restaurant a success from the growing and transporting of the food to the preparing and serving of the meal. Try to list one of these occupations for each letter of the alphabet.

8. SOCIAL STUDIES:
Cultural Diversity
In your own words, tell which types of ethnic foods you would most likely find on menus from each of the following cultures or locations represented in the United States: New England, Midwest, Deep South, Northwest, Southwest, Mexican, Jewish Delicatessen, Japanese Steak House, and Greek Taverna.

9. ALL SUBJECT AREAS:
Evaluation
Suppose you were rating each of the restaurants with their corresponding menus for a Golden Spoon Award. Would you give each one in your collection a one, two, or three star rating? Give 3-5 reasons for your choice in each case.

10. ALL SUBJECT AREAS:
Creative Writing
Design a menu for an original restaurant that has a specific theme reflecting one of the ideas listed below. Be sure your menu has a special name, color, shape, size, titles for food offerings, and a slogan or logo celebrating its decor. Consider each of the following options.

LANGUAGE ARTS THEME:
- A Menu with a Literary Theme
- A Menu with a Communication Theme

MATHEMATICS THEME:
- A Menu with a Geometry Theme
- A Menu with a Code or Cipher Theme

SOCIAL STUDIES THEME:
- A Menu with a Patriotic Theme
- A Menu with a Medieval Times Theme

SCIENCE THEME:
- A Menu with a Dinosaur Theme
- A Menu with an Ecology/Environmental Theme

A CALENDAR OF INTEGRATED LEARNING ACTIVITIES TO REINFORCE THE USE OF CHARTS AND TABLES

	Monday	Tuesday	Wednesday	Thursday	Friday
KNOWLEDGE COMPREHENSION	Use magazines and newspapers to find a wide assortment of charts and tables. State the main purpose or type of information given in each chart or table.	List all the different ways you can think of that we use tables and/or charts in our everyday lives. Consider how they are used in department stores, in airports, in supermarkets, and in sports.	Define table and chart, using a dictionary.	Take the information in one of the charts or tables and rewrite it in another form.	Classify your collection of charts and tables in at least three different ways. Explain the rationale for your grouping.
COMPREHENSION APPLICATION ANALYSIS	Compare a chart and a table. In a good paragraph, summarize how they are alike and how they are different.	Collect information about junk foods popular with your age group. Show your findings in chart form.	Construct a chart to show how you would like to spend a perfect 24-hour day.	Survey the students in your class to determine their favorite television show. Show your results on a chart.	How is a chart or a table like a road map? like a blueprint? like a photograph?
ANALYSIS SYNTHESIS	Study your collection of charts and tables. Determine some types of data and subject matter that are best depicted by a chart or table.	Diagram a flow chart for constructing a graph or a table on grade point averages for students in your math class.	Write a story that has one of the following titles: "The Magic Chart" "Couldn't Believe That Table" "What Happened To That Chart?" "The Missing Table" "Charts Can Make A Difference"	What do you think these common expressions mean? a. He turned the tables on me! b. Let's chart your course for the rest of the school year.	Design a poster about a school project, event, or activity that uses a chart or table as part of its message.
EVALUATION	Develop a set of recommendations for students to follow when constructing high-quality charts or tables.	Develop a set of criteria for judging the worth or value of a given chart or table. Apply this criteria to each unit of your collection. Rank order your charts and tables, from the most effective to the least effective.	Defend this statement: Presenting a chart or table is the BEST way to convince a friend of something.	Design a poster of charts or tables. Find as many different examples as you can. Mount examples on posterboard and write three insightful questions about each one.	Explain how each of the following people might use tables and/or charts in their work: pilot, scientist, stockbroker, supermarket manager, doctor.
EVALUATION	Explain the kinds of charts each of the following persons might construct for use in his or her chosen career or field of study: teacher, textbook publisher, history student, mapmaker.				

244

A CALENDAR OF INTEGRATED LEARNING ACTIVITIES TO PRESENT DIFFERENT FORMS OF POETRY

	Monday	Tuesday	Wednesday	Thursday	Friday
INTRODUCING POETRY	Choose a book of poetry. Use it to write down titles, author/editor, illustrator, copyright, some common subjects for poems, some unusual titles of poems, and methods used for grouping or organizing the poems.	Choose a poem you like, write it down, and draw a picture to illustrate it.	Compile a poetry word bank to use in your own writing. Try to find colorful words that describe: size, shape, condition, motion, sound, taste, texture, feelings, etc. Write them on file cards.	Pick a letter of the alphabet. Draw a large picture of the letter. Write a description and begin each line with the letter you chose.	Make up a tongue-twister following this model: First line is statement. Second line asks if statement is true. Third and Fourth lines ask an "if" and "where" question.
POETRY TERMS	Alliteration is the repeated use of the same sound. Decide on an object and write an alliterative sentence to describe it. Use your thesaurus for ideas.	Onomatopoeia is the use of words that sound like what they describe. Choose one of these sounds and illustrate it through a simple drawing using bright colors and a comic book style: buzz, whoosh, hiss, slurp, pssst, grrrrrr.	Similes are simple comparisons using the key words "as" or "like." Complete these comparisons using uncommon or unusual ideas: as ridiculous as . . . , as nutty as . . . , as nervous as . . . , as funky as . . .	A metaphor is a comparison to create a special image. It does not use the words "like" or "as." Metaphors usually state or imply that one object actually IS another object. Find several examples of metaphors in advertising.	Personification is the giving of human traits to non-human objects. Create an original personification idea of your own.
POETRY FORMS	Haiku is a form of Japanese poetry. It has three short lines, each expressing a lovely idea. The first line has 5 syllables, the second has 7, and the third has 5. Write an original haiku.	A diamante has 7 lines that describe a person or object. The pattern for writing a diamante is as follows: 1 noun or pronoun, 2 adjectives, 3 participles, 4 nouns, 3 participles, 2 adjectives, and 1 noun (synonym for first line). Create one of your own.	A free verse poem does not rhyme. Try making up one to share with the class.	Write a nonsense poem in which each word begins with a consecutive letter of the alphabet. You may make your lines of any length and you may start anywhere in the alphabet.	Find a limerick and note its rhyming pattern. Use it to create a limerick of your own.
POETRY PROJECTS	Create a poetry poster by choosing a theme, selecting poems and magazine pictures to represent your theme, and arranging them in an organized and creative way. Give your poster a title.	Choose three different poems on the same subject. Explain how these poems are alike and how they are different. Conclude which poet makes better use of imagery, rhyme, and content.	Write a GROUP POEM with any five of your classmates. Everyone writes one line of the poem following these rules: 1. Every line begins with "I wonder." 2. Every line has a color. 3. Every line names a person, place, or thing.	Create a poetry anthology around a popular theme—humor, holidays, nature, or heroes. Copy favorite poems from books, making certain to illustrate them in some way. Give your book a cover, title page, table of contents, and bibliography.	Invent a game about poetry. Make a gameboard, a set of game cards, and a set of rules. Include markers. Some ideas for game cards might be: Complete this simile . . . Say 5 words using alliteration . . . Describe the rhyming scheme for haiku . . .

SELECTED STUDENT RESPONSES TO POETRY CALENDAR

	Monday	Tuesday	Wednesday	Thursday	Friday
INTRODUCING POETRY				S nakes lip lowly ilently through wamps	Peter Piper picked a peck of pickled peppers. Did Peter Piper pick a peck of pickled peppers? If Peter Piper picked a peck of pickled peppers, where's the peck of pickled peppers Peter Piper picked?
POETRY TERMS	A horn in an orchestra can blare, blast, bleat, blow, blubber, bluff, or blurr with the conductor's blazing baton.				Auto: An auto is a public nuisance. It eats gas and spits water. It pollutes the environment. It deteriorates with age. Cars can throw you into a panic and traffic jams make drivers frantic!
POETRY FORMS	A spark in the sun, this tiny flower has roots deep in the cool earth.	NaCl Microscopic, Powdery Analyzing, Predicting, Testing Atom, Element, Molecule, Compound Heating, Cooling, Crystallizing, Necessary, Flavorful Salt	I am a kite, The king of the Sky. I drift lightly, I soar and dive. I value my freedom With the wind by my side.	Orangutans Prance Quickly Rescuing Stupid Tarantulas Under Varied, Wicked X-pressways Yelling Z-E-B-R-A.	
POETRY PROJECTS					

ASSESSING STUDENT INTERESTS, ABILITIES, AND GROWTH

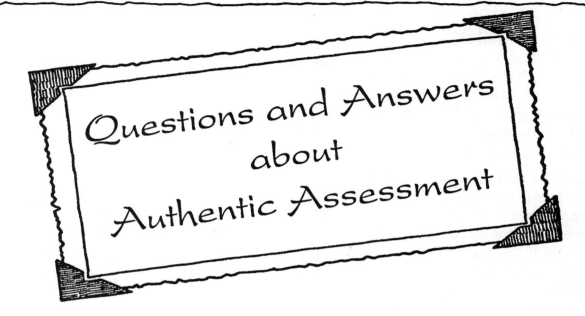

Questions and Answers about Authentic Assessment

1. What is authentic assessment?

Authentic assessment measures student achievement in a way that is as close to a real-life situation as the testing process allows. It is a type of assessment that requires the student to directly demonstrate a particular behavior or set of skills. This can be accomplished through the use of a portfolio, through the design and construction of a product, or through a student-generated demonstration or performance. It is NOT a standardized, contrived, regimented, step-by-step objective or traditional type of quiz, test, or exam.

2. What are some characteristics of authentic assessments?

In general, authentic assessment tools and techniques should display the following characteristics.

a. They are designed to be public, requiring some type of audience.
b. They are not bound by unreasonable time limits.
c. They do not contain secret questions or tasks unknown to the student in advance.
d. They encourage collaboration with others.
e. They contain a metacognitive dimension on the part of the student.
f. They empower the student in both design and their implementation.
g. They use a multi-faceted scoring system.
h. They build on a student's strengths.
i. They accommodate a student's learning style, interest, and aptitude.
j. They are cooperative rather than competitive.

3. What types of activities occur in authentic assessment measures?

Variety is encouraged when engaging in authentic assessment experiences. The experiences can include everything from work samples, self-assessment ratings, and observations to simulated performances, interviews, and prepared presentations.

4. What are the advantages and disadvantages of authentic assessment?

Authentic assessment is desirable because it integrates assessment with the curriculum; it is an active, not a passive, experience; it focuses on higher-order thinking skills; it encourages creativity; it broadens the testing content; and it nurtures interaction and communication between the students and their peers and teachers. Authentic assessment is also more time-consuming and expensive; it is more difficult to use on a widespread and large-scale basis; and it requires extensive training of faculty and students.

1. What is a portfolio?

A portfolio is one type of authentic assessment. It is a meaningful collection of student work that contains artifacts which exhibit the student's overall efforts, progress, and achievements in one or more related areas.

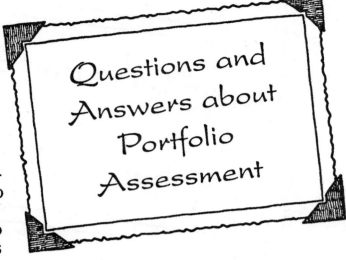

Questions and Answers about Portfolio Assessment

2. When does one use the portfolio assessment method?

There are several different types of portfolios and reasons for using portfolios to document student achievement. If the purpose is evaluation, then the portfolio should contain evidence of the student's best work. If the purpose is growth over time, then the portfolio should contain items representative of a student's work at various stages of his or her development in a subject area. If the purpose is to see how a student tackles a problem/task/challenge, then the portfolio should house a record of all student activities, drafts, revisions, and outcomes. It is important that the portfolio also contain several entries that are self-reflections and self-evaluations of the student's work.

3. What decisions have to be made when one implements the portfolio method of assessment?

There are five basic decisions that a teacher and student must consider when using portfolios in the classroom.

a. What physical structure, format, or organizational scheme will the portfolio take?

b. What types of evidence or artifacts will be included in the portfolio to best represent the student's abilities, interests, aptitudes, and accomplishments?

c. What types of timelines, assignments, tasks, and products should be used for documenting a student's progress?

d. What criteria, standards, benchmarks, or outcomes will be established to judge the value or worth of the portfolio contents?

e. What guidelines, methods, or procedures will be established for moving the portfolios on throughout a student's schooling years?

4. What kinds of things might go into a portfolio?

There are many different types of items that can be used in the portfolio system. These should be varied, current, reflective, and relevant to both the curriculum being taught and the instructional strategies being used. Some alternative artifacts might include:

a. Written assignments
b. Standardized, multiple-choice, and essay test questions/scores
c. Interest inventories
d. Teacher observations, interviews, and anecdotal records
e. Journal, diary, and learning log entries
f. Textbook assignments and tasks
g. Reading lists
h. Art, musical, and drama pieces
i. Performance notes, recordings, speeches, and presentations
j. Research findings, reports, and position papers

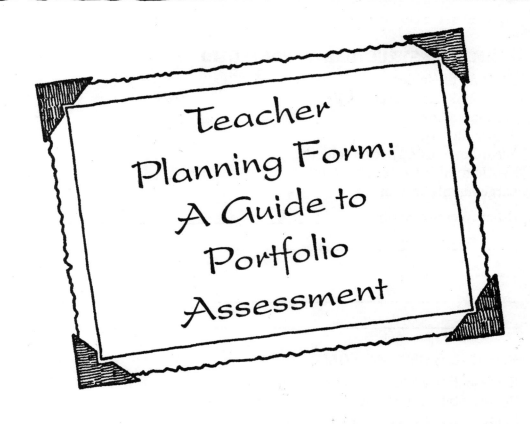

Teacher
Planning Form:
A Guide to
Portfolio
Assessment

In planning your classroom portfolio assessment program, use the outline below as an organizing tool for getting it started. Check all items that apply.

I. PURPOSE OF PORTFOLIO

___ Displaying and evaluating a collection of the student's best work
___ Showing student growth by means of a collection of representative work over a period of time
___ A collection of student's records, drafts, and revisions showing how he or she went about doing a specific and/or single project (metacognition)
___ Celebrating with a collection of student's work chosen by student alone
___ Aiding instruction by means of a collection of student drafts by which the teacher may determine student's progress
___ Some combination of above

___ Other (please describe) _____

_____

_____

_____

_____

_____

_____

_____

II. FORMAT OR STRUCTURE OF PORTFOLIO

___ Hanging file folder
___ Scrapbook of artifacts
___ Cardboard box
___ Plastic file case
___ Accordion pleated pocket folder
___ Plastic mini-briefcase or portfolio
___ Large manila envelope

___ Other (please describe) _____

_____

_____

_____

_____

III. CONTENTS OF PORTFOLIO

___ Representative classroom quizzes and tests
___ Representative standardized tests and instruments
___ Representative textbook assignments
___ Representative learning center activities
___ Representative independent study contract results
___ Representative reports and research findings
___ Representative homework assignments
___ Representative journal/diary/learning log entries

___ Other (please describe) _____

_____

_____

_____

_____

IV. METHODS OF CONTENT SELECTION

___ Selected by student
___ Selected by peers
___ Selected by teacher(s)
___ Selected by parents/guardians
___ Selected by combination of above

___ Other (please describe) _____

_____

_____

_____

_____

V. ALTERNATIVE SCHEDULES FOR CONTENT SELECTION

___ Selected daily
___ Selected weekly
___ Selected monthly
___ Selected quarterly or semi-annually
___ Selected annually
___ Selected combination of above

___ Other (please describe) _____

_____

_____

_____

_____

VI. METHODS FOR EVALUATION OF PORTFOLIO CONTENTS

___ Student self-evaluation
___ Peer review
___ Panel and/or other public audiences
___ Teacher
___ Checklists
___ Observations
___ Interviews
___ Anecdotal records
___ Prepared quizzes, tests, and exams
___ Standardized tests
___ Product development
___ Performances/presentations

___ Other (please describe) _____

_____

_____

_____

_____

VII. METHODS FOR PASSING ON PORTFOLIO CONTENTS

___ Student hand-carries to next year's grade/teacher/team leader
___ Teacher passes on to next year's grade/teacher/team leader
___ School passes on to next year's grade/teacher/team leader
___ Parent/guardian hand-carries to next year's grade/teacher/team leader

___ Other (please describe) _____

_____

_____

_____

Sample Student Portfolio for Mathematics

You will be collecting samples of your work in math class during the school year. Please follow these guidelines for putting together your mathematics portfolio.

1. Keep your work samples in the hanging file which the teacher has given you for this purpose.

2. Organize each work sample so that it is in chronological order. Make sure the date is on each item.

3. Select work samples for your portfolio that are representative of your growth in math over time during this semester and that are varied to show the different kinds of work that you do as part of this math class.

4. Try to include one math work sample for each week of the semester.

5. Once a month, plan to include one math work sample that you are very proud of and one that you wish had turned out better. Include written comments about these two selections.

MATH WORK SAMPLES TO INCLUDE IN YOUR PORTFOLIO

Directions: Check off those work samples which have been selected for this portfolio.

____ 1. My best math quiz, end-of-unit test, and take-home test
____ 2. Entries from my learning log on decimals (during month of October)
____ 3. A cooperative learning group activity on fractions
____ 4. Activities from the learning center on tangram geometry
____ 5. Report on "Symmetry"
____ 6. Representative word problems I know how to do
____ 7. My independent study contract for research on a famous mathematician
____ 8. Results from my "Math Interest Inventory"
____ 9. My best and worst math homework assignment
____ 10. My drafts of graphing project
____ 11. A letter to my next year's math teacher telling him or her about my strengths and weaknesses in mathematics

"Thinking about Thinking" Questions
Students Can Answer about Portfolio Assessments

1. What is the value of this portfolio for me? for my teacher? for my parents? for my peers?

_____

_____

_____

_____

2. What types of work will one find in this portfolio?

_____

_____

_____

_____

3. Who selected the pieces of work for this portfolio? How were they selected?

_____

_____

_____

_____

4. Why did I (or my teacher) select a particular piece of work for this portfolio? What did it represent?

_____

_____

_____

_____

5. What did I learn from a particular piece of work in this portfolio? Why was it important to me?

_____

_____

_____

_____

"Thinking about Thinking" Questions
Students Can Answer about Portfolio Assessments

6. If I could improve one piece of work in this portfolio, which one would it be and what would I change?

_____

_____

_____

_____

7. Which piece of work in this portfolio gave me the greatest satisfaction or pleasure? the greatest difficulty or frustration?

_____

_____

_____

_____

8. Which piece of work in this portfolio represents the best learning experience for me and why?

_____

_____

_____

_____

9. Which piece of work in this portfolio best represents how I learn best?

_____

_____

_____

_____

10. What types of work would I like to add to this portfolio in the future?

_____

_____

_____

_____

Name _____

Questions and Answers about Performance Assessment

1. What is performance assessment?

Performance assessments require that a student attempt to apply acquired information and skills to a new situation testing the student's ability to transfer rather than recall skills and knowledge. It relates to the higher levels of Bloom's Taxonomy beginning with the Application Level because a student must analyze, synthesize, and evaluate information in a context different from the one in which it was taught.

Performance assessments can follow many different formats ranging from the formal, highly structured test in which the student follows a prescribed exercise according to a given set of standards, outcomes, or criteria to one that is more flexible and spontaneous in which the teacher observes students during instruction according to a checklist of desired skills and concepts.

2. What are some of the benefits of performance assessment?

Performance assessments allow for more student creativity and self-expression than one finds in more traditional types of assessment. They encourage assessment that is active, situational, authentic, and/or contextual in its design. These performance assessments enable each student to demonstrate mastery in his or her own way just as long as one provides evidence that learning has taken place in a meaningful and significant way. Student input and teacher feedback are both integral parts of the performance assessment process. Students know well in advance the questions that will be asked, which skills will be tested, and which tasks will be demonstrated because they have had some ownership in their selection and design. And teachers have a variety of tools at their disposal to grade and judge the quality of the student performance ranging from formal scales and checklists to letter grades and personal comments.

3. What are some other unique features of performance assessment?

Performance assessments differ significantly from traditional and objective tests as we know them today. To begin with, when one constructs a performance exercise it does not involve writing a series of test items, but rather it consists of designing an assessment that relies more on a teacher's observation and professional judgment about what a student can and cannot do.

Furthermore, performance assessment tools and techniques stress higher-order thinking skills and not right or wrong answers. They feature hands-on or "learning by doing" instructional activities as opposed to paper-and-pencil outcomes. Finally, they rely on student exhibits and displays of knowledge and skills rather than knowledge-based multiple-choice or true-false questions.

4. How does one design a performance assessment?

There are a number of steps to be followed in designing a performance assessment. They include the following:

a. Deciding on the major student objectives, student performance standards, or student outcomes to be addressed.

b. Describing the decision, problem-solving, or performance situation in some detail.

c. Designing the set of testing tasks using graphics, visual clues, advanced organizers, and verbal directions in a clear and concise manner.

d. Outlining the desired student responses.

e. Selecting the rating procedures and providing some guiding criteria for their application.

DATE OF SCHEDULED PERFORMANCE: April 28

DATE OF VIDEOTAPE PRACTICE SESSION: April 26

TOPIC OF PERFORMANCE PRESENTATION:
An Oral History and Investigation Project on
Cultural Diversity Patterns in Your School

Sample Student Performance Assessment for Social Studies

TO THE STUDENT: You are to complete an oral history and investigation project on the cultural diversity patterns in your school based on interviews, school records, and other written sources and then present your findings orally in class. To accomplish this task, you are to create two workable hypotheses based on your preliminary investigations and three good questions you will ask to test each hypothesis. You are also to conduct at least three interviews of culturally diverse families represented in your school population.

TO THE TEACHER: When evaluating this oral history and investigation project on cultural diversity patterns in your school, consider the following criteria for grading:

1. Did the student establish two hypotheses?

2. Did the student develop three insightful questions to test each hypothesis?

3. Did the student select three culturally diverse families from the school to interview that are representative of the school community?

4. Did the student use school records in an appropriate way to test his or her hypotheses?

5. Did the student locate and use a wide variety of written sources to document his or her findings?

6. Did the student accurately depict the changes in student population which have occurred over time?

7. Did the student have follow-up questions to ask when answers were given to each hypothesis and each interview?

8. Did the student know the differences between facts and opinions in the answers given and the results found?

9. Did the student use evidence to document his or her best hypothesis?

10. Did the student demonstrate effective research, organization, and presentation skills?

Note: Use the following rubric rating scale to assign points for each of the above criteria in your evaluation process.   1 = Little or no evidence of this student skill/behavior/outcome.
2 = Some evidence of this student skill/behavior/outcome.
3 = Considerable evidence of this student skill/behavior/outcome.
4 = Significant evidence of this student skill/behavior/outcome.

Overall Grade *(circle one)*:
A *Excellent*   **B** *Very Good*   **C** *Good*   **D** *Needs Improvement*   **E** *Will Make Changes & Repeat*

Comments: _____

_____

_____

_____

_____

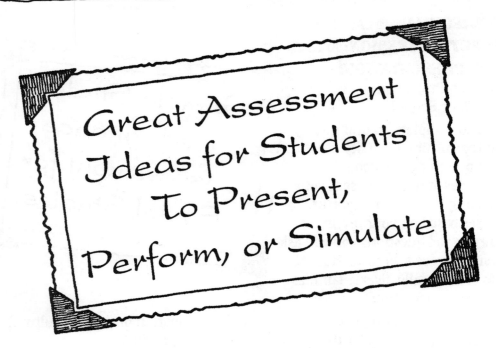

Great Assessment Ideas for Students To Present, Perform, or Simulate

1. Imagine you are a travel agent. Organize a travel agency complete with travel brochures, intercultural excursions, and unusual services for youth as clients.

2. Imagine you are a biologist. Create a new life form for an existing biome.

3. Imagine you are a newspaper publisher. Organize an editorial staff and publish a classroom, school, or neighborhood newspaper whose primary purpose is to inform and involve parents and community in the schooling process.

4. Imagine you are an economist. Create a mini-society for kids in the classroom that includes major government and privately owned services such as a bank, post office, city hall, police force, and series of retail outlets.

5. Imagine you are the CEO of a large public relations firm. Create a new product and develop a comprehensive marketing plan to sell it to the public.

6. Imagine you are an interior designer that specializes in the refurbishing and remodeling of schools. Develop a plan to make your school a more aesthetic and functional facility in which to play and learn.

7. Imagine you are a historian. Recreate a historical period and setting of your own choosing such as a pioneer village, a medieval kingdom, a western town, or a Roman city.

8. Pretend you are a museum curator. Decide on a "new and different" museum theme for today and design a series of museum exhibits and tours.

9. Pretend you are an international student leader. Create a mini United Nations for your school representing the multiple cultures in your local population.

10. Pretend you are a patron of the arts who admires and supports the art work of today's young people. Plan, organize, and implement an art gallery for your school or community that sponsors a wide variety of "art events" for students throughout the year.

11. Pretend you are an entrepreneur. Design and sponsor a special marketplace for your school where students can create products to sell and services to provide.

12. Pretend you are the head of a welcoming bureau for your school. Create a travel brochure making it sound like a great place to visit. Think about qualities, features, and sights that make a place interesting and try to find those same things in your school.

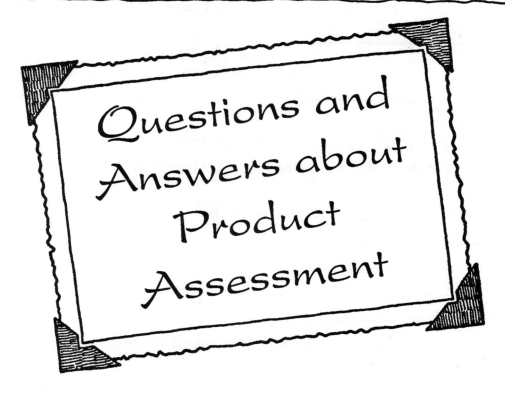

Questions and Answers about Product Assessment

1. What is product-based assessment?

Product-based assessment is an assessment that requires the student to produce evidence of achieved instructional goals that have taken place during a learning situation. This evidence takes the form of a concrete end result ranging from a display, videotape, or exhibit to an experiment, production, or manual.

2. What kinds of products are possible in product-based assessment?

Essays, stories, works of art, projects, displays, presentations, lectures, sketches, drafts, plans, articles, books, compositions, research results, experiments, models, theories, games, designs, notes, notebooks, study cards, photographs, pictures, videotapes, charts, graphs, maps, drawings, exhibits, tapes, discussions, drama, role play, dance, scrapbooks, news stories/reports, diaries, transparencies, oral reports, collections, guest speakers, letters, interviews, surveys, field trips, debates.

3. What is the difference between product-based assessment and performance-based assessment?

Product-based assessment emphasizes the product as an end result of a student's effort, as opposed to the process itself, which is the performance assessed in performance-based assessment. In accordance with authentic teaching, which stresses the future real-world application of in-class learning, the product of product-based assessment is related directly to the application of the subject area involved. For instance, in an English class, a novel or a book of poems would be an appropriate product for assessment, since novels and books of poetry are regularly required of authors in the field.

4. How does one go about designing a product-based assessment?

There are several steps required of the teacher when designing a product-based assessment.
  a. Limit the student to no more than three major skill and/or content objectives.
  b. Provide a list of possible product formats for students to consider.
  c. Establish guidelines for quality product construction and/or demonstration.
  d. Selecting criteria for judging worth of product.

"Thinking about Thinking" Questions Students Can Answer about Authentic Assessment Products

1. How much time did I spend on this project? How did I use the bulk of my time on this project?

   _____

   _____

   _____

   _____

2. Where did my ideas come from for this project? Which ideas seemed to work out better than others?

   _____

   _____

   _____

   _____

3. What problems did I encounter when working on this project? How did I go about solving them?

   _____

   _____

   _____

   _____

4. What kinds of help did I receive on this project?

   _____

   _____

   _____

   _____

5. What are the strengths of my work on this project? What are the parts of my project that seem to be weak?

   _____

   _____

   _____

   _____

"Thinking about Thinking" Questions Students Can Answer about Authentic Assessment Products

6. What do others seem to think of my project? How do I feel about their comments, suggestions, and criticisms? What changes did I make as a result of their input?

_____

_____

_____

_____

7. What things do I want the teacher to consider when judging or evaluating my project? What grade do I expect him or her to give me for this project?

_____

_____

_____

_____

8. What skills did I use in completing this project? What concepts did I learn in completing this project?

_____

_____

_____

_____

9. What were the most important outcomes for me in working on this project?

_____

_____

_____

_____

10. What things would I do differently next time when completing a project of this type?

_____

_____

_____

_____

Name _____

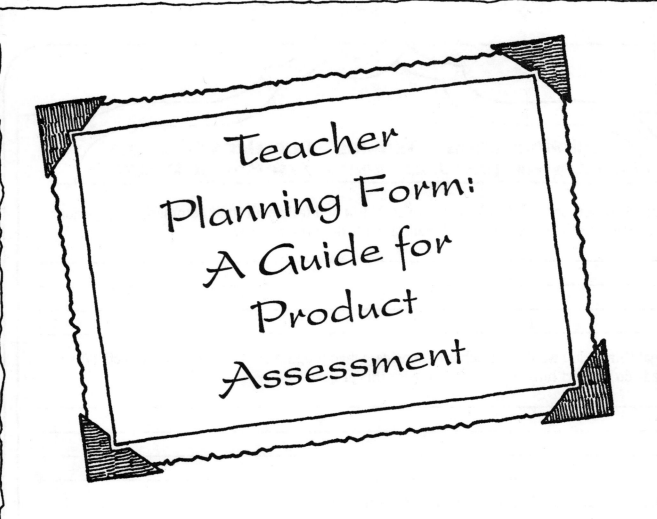

Teacher
Planning Form:
A Guide for
Product
Assessment

In assigning a product for authentic assessment purposes, it is important to keep the following guidelines in mind:

1. Provide students with a list of multiple project formats to consider. A list of possible options is outlined below.

2. Suggest to students that they select no more than two major skill objectives and no more than two major concept objectives to use in the design of their project. More than four objectives for any given project can lead to results that focus more on "quantity" of information and application rather than "quality" of information and application efforts. A list of possible skill objective options is listed below. Content objectives will vary according to subject matter.

3. Insist that students complete an outline or plan for completing their projects before they get started. A sample is found on page 266.

4. Establish criteria for assessing the worth of the project well in advance of project completion dates so that students know exactly what is expected of them. A list of possible evaluation criteria is listed on the next page.

MULTIPLE PROJECT FORMATS

Tape recording
Diagram or flow chart
Pamphlet
Newspaper
Bulletin board
Scale model
Display
Exhibit
Learning center
Movie scroll
Mini-textbook
Scroll
Collection of
    charts/graphs

Gallery/museum
    showcase
Choral reading
Book cover
Project cube
Photo-picture essay
Television script
Editorial
Debate/panel
    presentation
Position paper
Series of commercials/
    advertisements
Shoebox picture shows

Brochure
Commemorative plates/
    stamps/pop-up cubes
Movie script
Music video
Memoirs
Slide show
Time capsule
Children's book
Computer program
Shadow box
Timeline
Videotape
Newsletter

POSSIBLE SKILL OBJECTIVES

Classify
Compare and contrast
Generalize
Summarize
Describe
Demonstrate
Apply
Draw conclusions
Discover
Examine
Investigate

Predict
Translate
Analyze
Deduce
Infer
Uncover
Combine
Design
Develop
Invent
Produce

Synthesize
Argue
Criticize
Critique
Defend
Judge
Justify
Recommend
Test
Validate

POSSIBLE ASSESSMENT CRITERIA

Knowledge of concept
Application of skill
Organization of information
Presentation of information
Correct use of grammar
Correct use of punctuation
Creative format
Creative presentation of ideas
Creative use of information

Design of project format
Use of multiple resources
Documentation of information
Use of higher-order thinking skills
Flow of information
Topic of interest to others
Quality plan of action
Use of fact versus opinion
Ability to follow directions

Sample Student Product Assessment for Science

You are to create an ABC Book on a science topic of your choice. To complete this project, select your topic and then write down a related concept, term, event, or person for that topic next to each of the alphabet letters listed below. It is important that you have a key idea beginning with each letter to show what you have learned or know about that topic. Be sure that your booklet has a Title Page, a Dedication Page, a Table of Contents, a Bibliography, and a series of graphics, symbols, charts, graphs, diagrams, or visual images to illustrate each of your alphabet pages.

TOPIC FOR SCIENCE ABC REPORT: _____

DATE SCIENCE ABC REPORT IS TO BE COMPLETED: _____

ABC IDEAS TO WRITE ABOUT:

A_____   N_____
B_____   O_____
C_____   P_____
D_____   Q_____
E_____   R_____
F_____   S_____
G_____   T_____
H_____   U_____
I_____   V_____
J_____   W_____
K_____   X_____
L_____   Y_____
M_____   Z_____

Name _____

Sample Teacher Evaluation Sheet for ABC Science Reports

COUNTRY "ABCs" GRADE SHEET

PARENT'S/GUARDIAN'S SIGNATURE BY ASSIGNED DATE ....(5) _____

USED TIME WELL IN MEDIA CENTER AND CLASSROOM ....(20) _____

COVER SHEET ....(10) _____

TABLE OF CONTENTS COMPLETED ....(10) _____

EVERY LETTER IN ALPHABET SHOWN ....(10) _____

APPROPRIATE PAGES NUMBERED ....(5) _____

REQUIRED FACTS INCLUDED ....(20) _____

COMPLETED ENTRIES ....(1 PT. EA. = 30) _____

ILLUSTRATION FOR EACH ENTRY ....(1 PT. EA. = 30) _____

SPELLING/NEATNESS ....(10) _____

CREATIVITY ....(15) _____

TURNED IN ON TIME ....(5) _____

TOTAL ....(170) _____

BONUS—AN ENTRY FOR ALL 26 LETTERS ....(5) _____

COMMENTS: _____

_____

_____

_____

_____

Creative Report Formats as Possible Assessment Products

It is important to provide students with a wide variety of "reporting formats" when asking them to do research and write their findings. Below are several models that might help your students to structure their information in new and different ways.

REPORT FORMAT ONE:

Using "Bloom's Taxonomy" as a Report Format

Encourage your students to use Bloom's Taxonomy and its corresponding behaviors as a method for organizing their ideas. Some examples of "book report" outlines are shown below. This structure can also be used for "content reports."

A BOOK REPORT FOR HISTORICAL FICTION

KNOWLEDGE:.............What is the setting of this story?

COMPREHENSION:...Give examples of events and situations in this story that document the historical period represented in the setting.

APPLICATION:............Construct a timeline of the important events that make up the plot of the story.

ANALYSIS:....................Make a list of the characters in the story and classify your list in some way.

SYNTHESIS:.................Imagine you could spend a day with the main character of the story. What would you plan to see and do?

EVALUATION:..............Develop a rating scale and a set of criteria for judging a good book. Then determine the value of this book for other students your age using your scale and criteria.

A BOOK REPORT FORM FOR A BIOGRAPHY

KNOWLEDGE:..............List as many words as you can from the story that describe the main character. Include the page number for each.

COMPREHENSION: ...Describe several of the problems in the story that confronted the main character.

APPLICATION:............Write out a set of questions you would like to ask the main character of the story if you could interview him or her at this time.

ANALYSIS:....................Compare and contrast the main character of the story with a modern-day hero of similar background, sex, or occupation.

SYNTHESIS: ....Design a monument, trophy, award, or tombstone for the main character of the story.

EVALUATION:..............Based on what you know about the main character of the story, create a better title for the book and give reasons for your decision.

A BOOK REPORT FORM FOR A CHILDREN'S PICTURE BOOK

KNOWLEDGE:..............Give the title, author, publisher, and copyright date of this book.

COMPREHENSION: ...Summarize the content of the story in this book.

APPLICATION:............Practice reading this story aloud so that you can do so with accuracy, feeling, and clarity. Tape record your story-telling and share with students in primary grades.

ANALYSIS:....................Determine why this book has appeal for adult readers as well as young readers.

SYNTHESIS: ....Write an original book review for this story. Include it with a copy of your tape recording to make a "story-book package" to share with primary students.

EVALUATION:..............Decide whether this book could (or should be) a Newbery Award-winning story. Defend your position.

A BOOK REPORT FORM FOR A HOW-TO BOOK

KNOWLEDGE:..............Write down the author's main purpose in writing this book as well as three of the chapter titles that had a special interest for you. Write a one-sentence summary of the content for each of these chapters.

COMPREHENSION: ...Describe the type of person(s) who would benefit most from reading this book.

APPLICATION:............Choose three facts and three opinions from this book.

ANALYSIS:....................Compare and contrast this book with another book on the same topic. How are the books alike and how are they different?

SYNTHESIS: ....Suppose that you were to author a new book on this topic. Create an original book jacket for your new "best seller."

EVALUATION:..............Critique the visuals used in this book to enhance the information given. Were they effective? Give three to five reasons for your conclusion.

REPORT FORMAT TWO:
Using the "Alphabet or Number System" as a Report Format

Another useful way to organize report information is by using the letters of the alphabet or the numerals of our numbering system. Each letter of the alphabet, for example, can provide the foundation for writing a fact that begins with that letter or highlights a concept suggested by that letter. A report of 26 short paragraphs is the end result. In a similar fashion, the numerals 1 through 10 can serve as the organizers of ten short paragraphs using the appropriate number figure. For example, if a student were writing a report about "Germany," then he might start out a series of paragraphs using these statements as possible topic sentences: The single most important government leader in Germany is . . .; Two of the largest cities in Germany are . . .; Three historical landmarks that every visitor should see in the German countryside would be . . . , etc.

REPORT FORMAT THREE:
Using the How? What? When? Where? Who? and Why? Questions as a Report Format

In this format, each question provides the student with an opportunity to record information about a single topic or to record information about many topics. For example, a one-page report of six paragraphs could be written on a single subject as long as each paragraph answers one of the questions **how, what, when, where, who,** and **why.** An alternative might be to use each question as the springboard for writing about several different things as long as each paragraph answers one of the six questions. For example, a "WHY" report might answer the questions: "Why do things that go up always come down?" or "Why do leaves change colors in the fall?" or "Why do camels have humps?" or "Why does the tide go in and out?" The questions can all be centered around a common theme such as "weather" or they can be centered around a variety of topics unrelated to one another.

REPORT FORMAT FOUR:
Using the "What's So Important About" Phrase as a Report Format

Each line of this report format contains a simple statement of clarification and an illustration to highlight a point. It requires little writing, but can convey much information. For example, if your topic is "What's So Important About the Revolutionary War?" then each concluding idea can state a fact about the war with a final statement that clarifies the most important thing about the war.

REPORT FORMAT FIVE:
Using "What Is a Person, Place, or Thing?" Question as a Report Format

Each page of this report format is about a single topic and begins with the same topic sentence. Each paragraph of the report gives descriptive detail about the topic of discussion. For example, if the title of the report is "What Is A Flower?" each paragraph begins with the statement: "This is . . ." Descriptive sentences then follow which describe the object, such as: "This is an iris lily, a garden flower that is grown from bulbs."

REPORT FORMAT SIX:
Using the Textbook Chapter as a Report Format

Students write a mini-textbook chapter on a topic of their choice. They follow the standard textbook format used in their own science, math, or social studies resource making certain that the copy includes such traditional elements as chapter headings and subheadings, illustrations and graphs or diagrams, guiding questions, sidebar pieces of information, vocabulary charts, and an end-of-chapter quiz.

Diagrams

MY THOUGHTS ABOUT DIAGRAMS: Using the back of this paper, complete each of the following starter statements.

1. A dictionary definition of a diagram is . . .

2. Diagrams are used in textbooks to . . .

3. A diagram is often helpful to me when . . .

4. I wish someone would draw a diagram of . . .

5. A diagram is like a road map because . . .

DIAGRAM APPLICATION PROJECTS FOR ME TO DO

Diagrams can be very useful tools in understanding big ideas. Try constructing a diagram in one of these areas:

LANGUAGE ARTS
A Diagram of a Complex or Compound Sentence

SOCIAL STUDIES
A Diagram Depicting a Battle Strategy

MATH
A Diagram of a Mathematical Process

SCIENCE
A Diagram of a Chemical and Physical Change

Name _____

Examinations

MY THOUGHTS ABOUT EXAMINATIONS (TESTS): Using the back of this paper, complete each of the following starter statements.

1. Exams in schools are or are not (circle one) important to a student's progress because ...

2. Teachers often use exams to ...

3. I think a fair exam is one which ...

4. The best way to study for an exam is ...

5. One important piece of advice I would give my teacher about exams is ...

EXAMINATION APPLICATION PROJECTS FOR ME TO DO

Writing a good exam to test what a person knows or doesn't know is never an easy job. Try your hand at test-writing by designing a set of questions for one of the following areas.

LANGUAGE ARTS
Reference Materials in the Library or Media Center

SOCIAL STUDIES
Branches of Government

MATH
Geometric Figures and Formulas

SCIENCE
Scientific Method and Safe Laboratory Procedures

Name _____

Experiments

MY THOUGHTS ABOUT EXPERIMENTS: Using the back of this paper, complete each of the following starter statements.

1. It is necessary for people to experiment with new ideas and materials because . . .

2. The most important experiment I have studied or heard about recently is . . .

3. Sometime I would like to experiment with the notion that . . .

4. Many kids experiment with drugs, sex, or alcohol because . . .

5. People who enjoy the challenge of experimentation seem to be . . .

EXPERIMENT APPLICATION PROJECTS FOR ME TO DO

Conduct a simple experiment of your own to show something about one of these topics:

LANGUAGE ARTS
The Impact Television Has on the Reading Habits of Kids

SOCIAL STUDIES
What Influences Eating Patterns of Kids

MATH
The Factors That Most Affect the Attitude of Kids toward Math

SCIENCE
The Brand of Teenage Product (Shampoo, Lipstick, Hair Spray, Mouthwash, Toothpaste, etc.) That Is of Highest Quality

Name _____

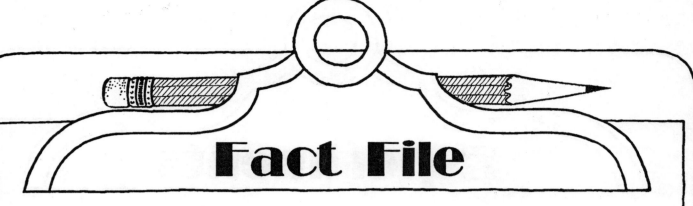

Fact File

MY THOUGHTS ABOUT A FACT FILE: Using the back of this paper, complete each of the following starter statements.

1. A fact differs from an opinion in that . . .

2. The expression "the fact of the matter is" suggests that . . .

3. A fact that distresses me is . . .

4. A textbook fact that I find very interesting is . . .

5. A fact that I want people to know about me is . . .

FACT FILE APPLICATION PROJECTS FOR ME TO DO

Prepare a fact file on one of the topics suggested here. Put each fact on a separate file card and organize your collection of fact cards in some meaningful way.

LANGUAGE ARTS
A Fact File on the Origin of Words

SOCIAL STUDIES
A Fact File on Your State

MATH
A Fact File on Mathematical Formulas, Theorems, and Terms

SCIENCE
A Fact File on Volcanoes, Tornadoes, Hurricanes, and Earthquakes

Name _____

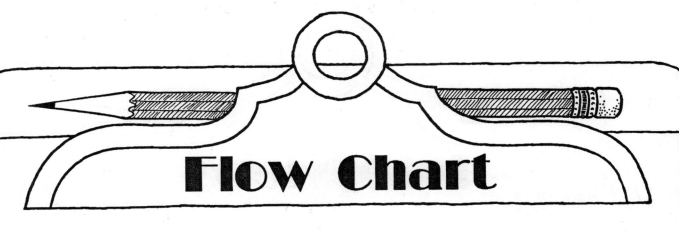

Flow Chart

MY THOUGHTS ABOUT FLOW CHARTS: Using the back of this paper, complete each of the following starter statements.

1. A flow chart is designed to . . .

2. A flow chart can help in decision-making because . . .

3. The most difficult thing to do when creating a flow chart must be . . .

4. Flow charts are important to the use/understanding of computers because . . .

5. A flow chart is like a map in that . . .

FLOW CHART APPLICATION PROJECTS FOR ME TO DO

Draw a flow chart to show one of these decision-making processes using the symbols suggested here: → ○ → ◇ ↑ □ ↓ ↔

LANGUAGE ARTS
Selecting a Book To Read Aloud to Young Children

SOCIAL STUDIES
Locating the Shortest Distance Between Two Points on a Map

MATH
Choosing Operations for Solving a Word Problem

SCIENCE
Identifying Common Birds, Reptiles, or Rocks

Name _____

Interviews

MY THOUGHTS ABOUT INTERVIEWS: Using the back of this paper, complete each of the following starter statements.

1. Interviews are the best sources of information when you want to . . .

2. Someone I would like to interview is . . . because . . .

3. Three Dos and Don'ts of interviewing are . . .

4. An interview could best be used to gather data for a school report if . . .

5. I wish someone would interview me about my feelings on . . .

INTERVIEW APPLICATION PROJECTS FOR ME TO DO

Try your hand at interviewing by first writing out a list of 6 to 10 questions you would ask someone in an interview for one of the following situations.

LANGUAGE ARTS
An Interview with a Teenage Writer of Children's Books

SOCIAL STUDIES
An Interview with Twelve-Year-Old Twins Living in the White House

MATH
An Interview with a Child Prodigy in Mathematics

SCIENCE
An Interview with the World's First Kid in Space

Name _____

Journals

MY THOUGHTS ABOUT JOURNALS: Using the back of this paper, complete each of the following starter statements.

1. People like to keep journals of their daily activities, feelings, observations, or travels because . . .

2. Journals can preserve the history of a person or a period in time when . . .

3. Journals can help a person . . .

4. A famous person whose journal I would like to read if one were available is . . . because . . .

5. If I were to keep a regular journal I would most certainly want to write about . . .

JOURNAL APPLICATION PROJECTS FOR ME TO DO

Try your hand at journal writing by completing one of the hypothetical journal settings suggested here. Write a series of short but meaningful paragraphs for a week's time.

LANGUAGE ARTS
A Week in the Life of Tom Sawyer
A Week in the Life of Mother Goose

SOCIAL STUDIES
A Week in the Life of Harriet Tubman
A Week in the Life of Paul Bunyan

MATH
A Week in the Life of a Stockbroker on Wall Street
A Week in the Life of a Numbers Racketeer

SCIENCE
A Week in the Life of Thomas Edison
A Week in the Life of a Mad Scientist

Name _____

N is for Notes

MY THOUGHTS ABOUT NOTES: Using the back of this paper, complete each of the following starter statements.

1. Students take notes when they want to . . .

2. Taking notes in class is important because . . .

3. Good notes require that you . . .

4. A good way to study your notes from class is to . . .

5. The most difficult thing for me in note taking is . . .

NOTE TAKING APPLICATION PROJECTS FOR ME TO DO

Use the format shown here to take at least 5 to 10 different notes from an encyclopedia for a two-page report on one of the suggested topics.

TOPIC: _____

MAIN IDEA: _____

TWO DETAILS TO REMEMBER:

_____

_____

SOURCE: _____

LANGUAGE ARTS	**MATH**	**SOCIAL STUDIES**	**SCIENCE**
Hieroglyphics	Math Careers	Gladiators	Weather Instruments
Calligraphy	Calendars	California Gold Rush	Biomes

Name _____

Questionnaire

MY THOUGHTS ABOUT QUESTIONNAIRES: Using the back of this paper, complete each of the following starter statements.

1. A questionnaire is good for gathering data because . . .

2. One limitation of a questionnaire as a source of information is . . .

3. One area in which questionnaires are often used is to . . .

4. A good questionnaire should have . . .

5. A questionnaire I once responded to was about . . .

QUESTIONNAIRE APPLICATION PROJECTS FOR ME TO DO

Design a questionnaire of 6 to 8 questions to gather information of interest in one of your classes. Compile your findings in some way to share them with the group: chart, graph, report, poster, skit, etc.

LANGUAGE ARTS
Discover the most common writing errors of your classmates.

SOCIAL STUDIES
Discover the most common geography misunderstandings of your classmates.

MATH
Discover the most common mistakes on math tests.

SCIENCE
Discover the most common safety violations your classmates commit during science labs.

Name _____

Rating Scales

MY THOUGHTS ABOUT SCALES: Using the back of this paper, complete each of the following starter statements.

1. The purpose of a rating scale is . . .

2. Rank order means to . . .

3. Ratings are used to judge many things such as . . .

4. Some optional ways to organize numbers, rankings, and descriptors on a rating scale are . . .

5. As a student I would rate a _____ on a scale of _____ because . . .

RATING SCALE APPLICATION PROJECTS FOR ME TO DO

Practice designing and using a variety of different rating scales in some of the ways suggested below.

LANGUAGE ARTS
Determine the most popular literary characters and/or authors in your English/reading class. Develop a rating scale and rank order each one.

SOCIAL STUDIES
Determine the parts of the world most intriguing to your classmates. Develop a rating scale and rank order each one.

MATH
Determine the most significant contribution of the computer to our society as suggested by your math peers. Develop a rating scale and rank order each one.

SCIENCE
Determine the main causes of pollution as identified by your fellow students. Develop a rating scale and rank order each one.

Name _____

Tape Recordings

MY THOUGHTS ABOUT RECORDINGS: Using the back of this paper, complete each of the following starter statements.

1. Audiotapes and tape recorders are a great invention because . . .

2. Audiotapes would make a great learning tool if . . .

3. Audiotapes will most likely never replace textbooks since . . .

4. I wish someone would create an audiotape series on _____ because . . .

5. The most difficult thing to do well in making a high-quality audiotape must be . . .

TAPE RECORDING APPLICATION PROJECTS FOR ME TO DO

Make a short 3- to 5-minute audiotape for one of the listed subject areas. Include a set of follow-up questions for others to answer after listening to the content of your tape.

LANGUAGE ARTS
Tape record a series of poems on the same theme or topic from a variety of poetry books.

SOCIAL STUDIES
Tape record a series of newspaper articles on the same current event.

MATH
Tape record a series of word problems and suggestions on how to solve them.

SCIENCE
Tape record a difficult section of a chapter in your textbook.

Name _____

DIRECTIONS FOR BOOKBINDING

MATERIALS NEEDED

- cardboard, 6½" x 9½"
- rubber cement
- wallpaper, 7" x 11"
- needle
- dental floss
- ditto paper, 8½" x 11"
- construction paper, 9" x 12"
- cloth tape
- vinyl plastic letters

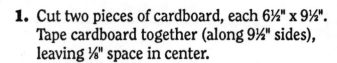

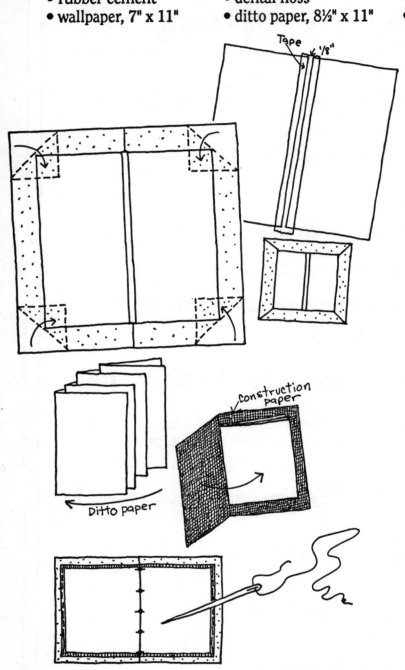

1. Cut two pieces of cardboard, each 6½" x 9½". Tape cardboard together (along 9½" sides), leaving ⅛" space in center.

2. You will need two pieces of paper to cover the cardboard, each piece 7" x 11". You can use wallpaper, cloth, contact paper, a painting, etc.

3. Open cardboard, taped side down. Glue cover paper to cardboard. Cover paper should touch edge of cardboard in center. Leave equal overhang, top and bottom. Fold overhang and glue onto cardboard. Do the corners first, and then the sides.

4. Fold four pieces of ditto paper (one at a time) in half to form 5½" x 8½" rectangles. Put them together, one inside the other. Fold one piece of construction paper into a 6" x 9" rectangle. Put this evenly around the four folded sheets.

5. Open your booklet flat. Mark the midpoint on the fold. Make two marks 1" from the ends of the cover paper. Make a mark halfway between each end mark and the midpoint. Poke holes through all thicknesses at marks.

6. Thread a needle with dental floss (about 20" long). Beginning at the back of the construction paper at the center fold, sew along pattern of holes.

7. Open cover. Glue construction paper to inside front and back covers. Put another piece of tape on the outside of the book (spine).

STEPS TO FOLLOW
TO FINISH MY PROJECT

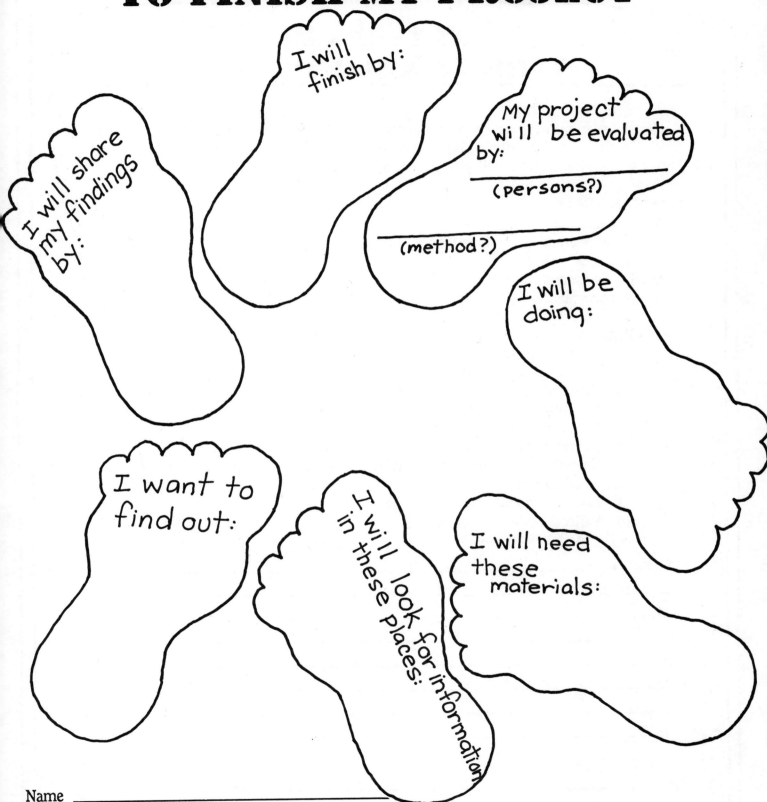

I will finish by:

I will share my findings by:

My project will be evaluated by:
_____
(persons?)

_____
(method?)

I will be doing:

I want to find out:

I will look for information in these places:

I will need these materials:

Name _____

From *The Teacher's Planning Pak and Guide to Individualized Instruction* by Imogene Forte and Joy MacKenzie. Nashville, TN: Incentive Publications, Inc., 1978.

© 1994 by Incentive Publications, Inc., Nashville, TN.

Self-Evaluation
Form To Assess My Work

Take a few minutes to review your finished product or presentation outline (or practice tape). Use the following criteria and scale to assess your work, or you may wish to devise both a set of criteria and a rating or grading scale to assess your work.

GRADING SCALE
A = Outstanding
B = Above Average
C = Average
D = Below Average
E = Not Acceptable

CRITERIA
___ **1.** Organization and clarity of information presented
___ **2.** Quality of content presented
___ **3.** Creativity and variety of ideas presented
___ **4.** Care and attention to detail
___ **5.** Use of multiple resources in developing ideas
___ **6.** Degree of interest, relevance, and value for audience
___ **7.** Correct use of grammar, vocabulary, punctuation, and/or syntax
___ **8.** Quality of visuals
___ **9.** Energy and enthusiasm for topic
___ 10. Reflects best efforts of student

Comments: _____

_____

_____

_____

_____

_____

_____

_____

Name _____

Peer Evaluation
Form To Assess the Work of Others

After examining a product or viewing a presentation (performance or demonstration) of another individual or group in your class, take a few minutes to complete this evaluation in order to give feedback on the work of your peers.

1. What was the theme, topic, or purpose of this product or presentation?

   _____

   _____

2. What two or three key ideas did you learn about the topic or theme from this product or presentation?

   _____

   _____

3. What part of the product or presentation did you think was the most creative, unusual, or unique?

   _____

   _____

4. What did the product developer(s) or presenter(s) do to capture the attention and interest of the audience?

   _____

   _____

5. What suggestions might you offer the product developer(s) or presenter(s) for improving and strengthening the work?

   _____

   _____

6. How would you rate the overall product or performance of this activity? You may assign a letter grade or a rating from a scale as long as you defend your position.

   _____

   _____

Name _____

Great Essay Topics for Students

MATHEMATICS

1. Write a number autobiography. Include numbers of special significance to you including such options as birth date, weight, height, address, telephone number, favorite radio station, bicycle registration number, or miles traveled during your summer vacation. Present this numerical data in a creative storytelling manner.

2. Compare and contrast the following items: a meter stick, a scale on a map, an odometer of a car, a tape measure, and a piece of string. How are they alike and how are they different?

3. What would happen if schools went out of business and children were taught at home using computers, videotapes, word processors, and other forms of advanced technology? Would children learn more or less?

4. Invent your own measurement system and describe how it works.

5. "Girls tend to have blue or green eyes and boys tend to have black or brown eyes." Develop a plan for testing this hypothesis in your classroom or school. Describe what you would do in detail and what results you would expect to find.

SCIENCE

1. Describe ways you have consumed natural resources during the last 24 hours both at home and at school.

2. Write non-stop for five minutes on the topic "Shoppers should have to bring reusable cloth bags to carry their groceries home from the supermarket if they wish to purchase any products."

3. If you were an alien from outer space and had to survive on the streets of a major American city, what would you need?

4. Society has many emotional issues that people feel strongly about. Some of these include abortion, organ banks, gay rights, and the slaughtering of the seals. Discuss the factors that cause people to feel so differently and so passionately about issues of this type.

5. Suppose you were given the challenge of creating a Five Senses time capsule for the year 2050. You have been instructed to include only a series of textures, smells, sights, sounds, and tastes that would be representative of the lifestyle of today's teenager. What things would you include?

Great
Essay Topics for Students, Page 2

6. If you were authorized to make a series of Academy Awards for the Insect Hall of Fame (or Reptile/Bird/Mammal Hall of Fame) describe what medals you would give to each of the following creatures and why.

    Insect That Is Most Resourceful
    Insect That Is Most Mysterious
    Insect That Is Most Misunderstood
    Insect That Is Most Beneficial To Mankind

7. Write down the name of your most prized and valuable possession. List several ways that science has contributed to its design, production, construction, or operation.

8. Discuss ways a microscope is like a pair of glasses, a mirror, a hand lens, and a telescope.

SOCIAL STUDIES

1. Discuss the cultural stereotypes that have created problems for different ethnic groups of people.

2. Write a detailed conversation between a rancher who has lost a large number of cattle from his ranch due to an outbreak of disease and an urban consumer who is refusing to buy "red meat" due to its high prices.

3. Give a woman who is running for President of the United States some good advice on what social issues to address, on what groups to visit, and what leadership traits to stress.

4. What do you feel are the five most important careers for young people to consider during the next decade? Give reasons for your answer.

5. Write a short diary entry describing your feelings in one of these historical situations or settings:

    a. An Afro-American slave during the Civil War
    b. A Jewish child in a concentration camp during World War II
    c. An Afro-American family moving into an all-white neighborhood during the 1960s
    d. A Japanese American in California after the bombing of Pearl Harbor
    e. An Hispanic immigrant in Miami during the Cuban missile crisis

Great
Essay Topics for Students, Page 3

6. Describe someone from the American Revolutionary War period that you feel was a hero who fought hard for a cause. Then think of someone in our country today who is also fighting for a common cause. What character traits do these individuals seem to have in common?

7. Discuss ways the United States is different from any European country from which many American immigrants have come.

8. Explain the Law of Supply and Demand and give a series of regional examples to support your explanation.

LANGUAGE ARTS

1. Imagine you have the responsibility of educating someone from outer space who has never encountered a skateboard. Describe it in detail.

2. Discuss the difference between a fact and an opinion. Choose a topic you feel strongly about and give three facts and three opinions about it.

3. Make a list of language arts topics about which you know quite a lot. Then select one of them and write about it.

4. An adjective is a descriptive word that can be an important part of every good sentence. Think of at least ten adjectives to describe your favorite character from a novel (read by the class). Use these adjectives to write a short character sketch.

5. Pretend you have been asked to create a very unusual and interesting alphabet or number book for young children. Select five letters from the alphabet or five numbers between 1 and 20 and design five pages for this book as a sampler to show a potential publisher.

6. Use your creative talents to write a series of three poems about a common object of your choosing. Title it: "Three Ways To Look At A _____." Write a haiku, a diamante, and a short rhyming verse about that object.

7. Write a sample page from the journal of your favorite author who has had a very productive day in writing a chapter for one of his or her existing novels that you have read. Be specific in your comments.

Ten Non-Traditional Ways To Assess Traditional Content

1. Design a test using Bloom's Taxonomy. You can design a test with only six questions, one for each level of the taxonomy. Assign points so that satisfactory completion of the test equals 100 points, but with varied points assigned to each level. A suggested point value system might be: Knowledge Question = 5 points; Comprehension Question = 10 points; Application Question = 15 points; Analysis Question = 20 points; Synthesis Question = 25 points; and Evaluation Question = 25 points.

   Another way to use Bloom's Taxonomy as an organizational structure in designing tests is to generate several questions at each level of the taxonomy and then allow students to choose which questions to answer. Again, the questions carry a point value at each level and students must answer any combination of questions that have a combined value of 100 points. Students cannot answer questions totaling more than 100 points (in case they miss some) because they must learn to make wise decisions when given choices and learn to live with the consequences of those decisions and choices.

2. Design a test that is kinesthetic and open-ended. In this case the test consists of 20 different concepts, facts, or terms associated with a given content area that the teacher considers most relevant to the unit of study. Each item is listed in one of 20 boxes on an 8½" x 11" sheet of paper. Instruct students to: (1) Tear worksheet into 20 sections (2) Group or classify sections in some way so that there are at least three groups (but there can be more) (3) List groups and group members (the concepts, facts, or terms) on a separate piece of paper (4) Write a brief summary statement that describes what each member of the group has in common with every other member of the group (rationale for classification system) (5) Write a paragraph for each group that demonstrates an understanding of the concepts represented by the members of that group, using factual information from class readings, discussions, lectures, activities, and assignments. Following are suggested guidelines for grading this testing format.

SCORING

1. **1.** Two or more groups: 10 points (knowledge)
2. **2.** Good list of group members: 10 points (knowledge)
3. **3.** Student describes relationship of members of each group according to some logical system: 20 points (comprehension)
4. **4.** Concepts represented by group members are accurate and defensible based on factual information obtained from readings/lectures/discussions/experiences, are consistent in their logic, and are comprehensive in their explanation and validation: 50 points (application/analysis/evaluation)
5. **5.** Groupings and/or descriptions demonstrate elements of creativity, innovativeness, or originality: 10 points (synthesis)

   NOTE: Points offered in numbers 4 and 5 can be changed to reflect higher value on creativity.

3. Design a test for a cooperative learning group. Administer the test to each individual within the group. Average the scores and give each member a grade that is the same as the group average. This strategy helps students better understand the importance of "tutoring" one another on the content of the test prior to its administration.

4. Design a "free association" test. This technique is one way to determine student perceptions and inferences about people, places, and things they have studied in a given unit. In this type of test, students are given a series of key names, concepts, dates, or events and are then asked to write down their initial ideas about each one as quickly as they can. They then must look over their written ideas and justify their choices.
Example: EGYPT: Sahara Desert — Camel — Nile River

5. Design a "what if" situational test. This technique is an excellent way to get students to project their thoughts and ideas into an imaginary setting. Students are given a set of "what if" statements and then are instructed to write down all possible implications of those statements.
Examples: What if the South had won the Civil War?
What if parents could determine the sex of their children?
What if it rained precious gems?

6. Design a "forced choice" test. Structuring a simple "forced choice" instrument can often provide the teacher with an opportunity to study student preference patterns in a given area.
Examples: Would you rather be a good leader or a good athlete?
Would you rather be an igneous or a metamorphic rock?
Would you rather have lived in medieval times or in colonial times?

7. Design a story or role-playing projective tool. Use a simple story, anecdote, or role-playing situation to help students clarify or understand their values, behaviors, or attitudes. Example:
Thomas Jefferson was very excited because he had just been elected President of the United States. He was walking down the muddy streets of Washington D.C. to his inau-

guration. He had deliberately kept the event simple because he felt his election was a victory for ordinary American citizens. He remembered a night when he had been talking with his wife in their plantation home. He had vowed that his goal as President was to make the government more democratic and more humane. Just as he was discussing how to accomplish this goal, an uprising occurred in one of the barracks housing his large number of slaves. Jefferson became very angry when one of the slave leaders asked him to improve the living conditions of black women and children on the plantation. He scolded the slave leader and told him to "mind his own business and get back to work harvesting sugar."

1. Do you think Thomas Jefferson had conflicting values as President of the United States? What makes you think so?
2. Do you think Thomas Jefferson regarded "blacks" in the same way as he did "ordinary American citizens"? Why or why not?
3. How would you feel if you were the slave leader?
4. What would you have done when the slave leader interrupted the conversation with your wife?

8. Design a "stump the experts" test. Have all students read a selection from a textbook, periodical, or reference book on a given subject. They are then to prepare about ten good questions to present to a student panel of experts. Select a panel of three class members to sit at the front of the class. Then the students ask their questions of the panel members, one at a time. All members of the panel are given a chance to answer the question should the first person asked be unable to do so. Questions are rotated so that no one person answers all of them. When every member on the panel fails to answer a given question, the panel may be retired or given a second chance. After the second miss by each panel member, a new panel is chosen and the process is repeated.

9. Design a "response card" quiz. Provide each student with five flash cards numbered one through five. Make yourself a set of flash cards on a given topic with five possible answers to a given question. Go through your series of questions, one card at a time, instructing students to choose the number from their card set that they think corresponds to the proper answer for each question asked. For example, if you were testing students on their understanding of elements of the periodic table, you might ask them this question:

The symbol for gold is written as:

1	2	3	4	5
Fe	G	Au	Cu	N

10. Design a test of "ambiguous" tasks that will challenge students to come up with creative responses.
    Examples: Draw a picture of political conflict.
    Explain combustion to a two-year old.
    Demonstrate infinity.
    Prove that the Earth is moving.
    Describe space.

TEACHER FORM: TALLY PROCESSING

Use the form below for recording group interactions. Write names of cooperative learning group members horizontally on the tally grid and the social processing skills to be observed vertically on the tally grid. When the observation period is completed, total number of tallies in both columns and rows. Show data to the group members and have them draw their own conclusions on the group's ability to function.

OBSERVATION TALLY GRID

Teacher's Name: _____

Group Task/Assignment: _____

Date: _____

	Student One	Student Two	Student Three
Disagreed in an agreeable way			
Took turns in speaking/listening			
Made clarifying statements			
Helped achieve group goals			
Stayed on task			
Offered assistance to group members			
Accepted assistance from group members			
Gave positive feedback to group members			

NOTE: Suggest that students rate themselves on each of the above social skills by using this type of scale:

How well did you . . . (stay on task, give positive feedback, etc.)

1......................2......................3......................4......................5

Not at all   Sometimes   All of the time

STUDENT ASSESSMENT SHEET: GRAPHING GROUP RESULTS

Use the graph below to discuss and reach group consensus on how well you worked together on the assigned task briefly described below:

TASK:

_____

_____

_____

	Stating Ideas (Knowledge)	Summarizing Ideas (Comprehension)	Applying Ideas (Application)	Analyzing Ideas (Analysis)	Creating New Ideas (Synthesis)	Critiquing Ideas (Evaluation)
More than I ever thought we could						
Most of the time						
Sometimes when we remembered						
Not nearly enough						
Forgot all about it						

Group _____

293

Student Evaluation Letter for Partner Activity

Write a letter to your partner telling him or her how you felt about working together and sharing your best ideas with one another during this activity.

Dear Partner,

Paragraph One: I want to thank you for . . .

Paragraph Two: I think your best ideas were . . .

Paragraph Three: I wish you could have told me more about . . .

Paragraph Four: The next time we work together I think we should . . .

Your friend,

Student Form:
Group Functioning Assessment

Complete each of the following questions as a group. Discuss each item before reaching a group consensus.

Group Members: _____

Group Task/Activity: _____

1. Did all of the group members contribute to achieving the group's goals?
   (Goal Interdependence: Establishing mutual goals)

   1....................... 2............................ 3............................ 4............................... 5
   Low   High

2. Did all of the group members do their share of the work?
   (Task Interdependence: Dividing labor)

   1....................... 2............................ 3............................ 4............................... 5
   Low   High

3. Did all of the group members share the group's resources?
   (Resource Interdependence: Dividing materials, tools, or information)

   1....................... 2............................ 3............................ 4............................... 5
   Low   High

4. Did all of the group members perform their group roles in an effective manner?
   (Role Interdependence: Assigning student jobs)

   1....................... 2............................ 3............................ 4............................... 5
   Low   High

5. Did all of the group members share in the end result?
   (Reward Interdependence: Giving joint rewards)

   1....................... 2............................ 3............................ 4............................... 5
   Low   High

EVIDENCE FOR ABOVE RATINGS: For each "Interdependence Rating" above, cite something a group member said or did that demonstrated your response.

Evidence for Goal Interdependence: _____

Evidence for Task Interdependence: _____

Evidence for Resource Interdependence: _____

Evidence for Role Interdependence: _____

Evidence for Reward Interdependence: _____

Fifteen "Testy" Ideas for Students To Act Upon

How would you respond to each of these "testy tasks"?

1. What would your class notes, tests, and quizzes say to your friends, parents, and teachers?

2. How can you infer what a teacher expects you to learn?

3. How is a test like a thermometer?

4. Survey 20 people to get their immediate reactions to the word "test." Graph the results in some way.

5. List your strengths and weaknesses as a test taker.

6. Design an ideal format for a better test.

7. On a test, when is remembering easy and forgetting difficult?

8. What makes a test fair? What makes a test worth taking?

9. Invent a new technique for evaluating what students know and don't know.

10. Create a test-taker's guide for students in your class.

11. Think of a question that has no right answer.

12. Rank order 15 careers in order of the need to memorize.

13. Create a "Jeopardy" game of answers. Administer your test and have peers come up with their best questions.

14. Design a "test-taking rally or pep assembly" for your class/school.

15. Organize a study group for taking tests. How will it function?

INDEX

ANSWER KEY

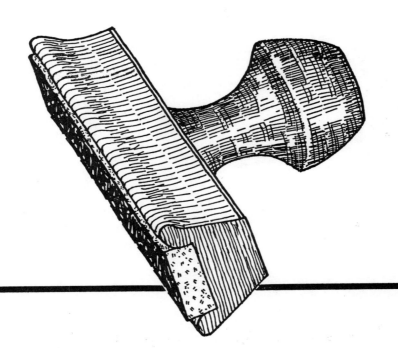

INDEX

299

ANSWER KEY

pp. 73-74

1. **Optical:** having to do with the sense of sight.
Illusion: unreal, misleading appearance.
Optical illusion: false perception of what one sees.

2. faces

3. The penny is closer. It blocks out the far-away moon, which leaves a much smaller image on the retina than does the nearby penny.

4. Answers may vary.

6. 1a. A looks larger than B.
1b. They are the same size.
2a. T looks larger than S.
2b. They are the same size.
3a. A looks as if it connects to C.
3b. B connects to C.
4a. E looks longer than D.
4b. D and E are the same length.

p. 97

U	I	E	W	S	M	A	E	T	R	I	O	I	S	L	O
O	K	P	A	C	I	F	I	C	I	S	L	A	N	D	S
A	L	I	K	T	D	T	L	E	A	L	L	Y	A	W	D
I	M	J	E	O	W	H	S	N	L	O	R	I	S	K	E
H	N	K	L	G	A	J	T	S	H	I	B	L	T	E	Y
M	O	D	E	R	Y	S	C	E	C	T	N	O	J	N	E
K	E	Y	E	L	T	H	R	E	T	E	R	M	O	A	C
T	X	O	A	C	N	E	O	D	U	Y	D	M	H	F	G
U	A	C	V	I	R	G	I	N	I	S	L	A	N	D	S
T	D	B	N	Q	J	V	X	T	O	X	S	M	Q	Y	Z
U	R	I	N	S	P	I	H	C	X	R	Z	P	O	A	R
I	A	Y	T	W	E	E	D	W	G	U	A	M	L	T	P
L	E	O	R	A	N	R	M	I	L	T	K	O	R	I	J
A	M	E	R	I	C	A	N	S	A	M	O	A	K	C	O
E	S	V	W	N	H	O	L	L	Y	X	U	N	I	N	R
Z	U	P	O	S	R	F	T	A	G	S	T	H	R	E	I

p. 98

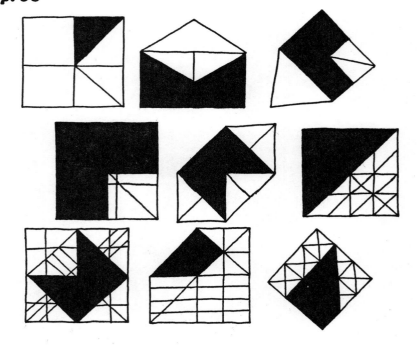

303